Getting Through!

Books by the same author:
A Guide to the Loire Valley
Boatopia
A Guide to Good English in the 1980s
Paris - the Essential City

Getting Through!

HOW TO
MAKE WORDS WORK

GODFREY HOWARD

DAVID & CHARLES
Newton Abbot   London

British Library Cataloguing in Publication Data

Howard, Godfrey
  Getting Through-how to make words work
  1. Verbal communication-Manual
  I. Title
  808'.042
  ISBN 0-7153-9410-X

First published 1989
Second impression 1989
Third impression 1990

Printed in Great Britain
by Billings & Sons Ltd
for David & Charles Publishers plc
Brunel House Newton Abbot Devon

For Françoise

CONTENTS

Introduction

Charles Saatchi started a modest advertising agency in London on the 14 September 1970 and within seventeen years turned it into the biggest advertising agency the world has ever known. He declared that although even he finds communication a 'very difficult subject', he greatly enjoyed reading *this book*. The Saatchi agency built its phenomenal success on new ideas and perhaps Mr Saatchi responded to this book because it is also about new ways of using words. The old approach starts off with the question 'What do I want to say?' If that is your way, as it is for most people, you will be introduced here to new attitudes which shift the focus to a much more important question: *What results do I want?* The difference this can make to your work and your life is astonishing.

Nearly every time you pick up your pen, sit down at a typewriter or wordprocessor, put your feet up and dictate to your secretary or into a recorder, telefax a letter across the world, go in to talk to the boss, rise to your feet in the House of Commons or address the nation from your desk in the White House, you are using words to make something happen.

Words can get you the job you want, get your complaint dealt with quickly and fairly, get you out of trouble, sell your car or your house, raise capital, increase sales, make someone do something or not do something, persuade a man or a woman to marry you or just have dinner with you. We know thousands of words in English plus the syntax of the language, how to combine those words into sentences. We can now move on to the next stage, which is how to make the best possible use of that knowledge in work and relationships, how to use words to get through to people.

9

INTRODUCTION

At school we learn vocabulary, spelling and grammar, and
are left to get on with the rest of it. It is like learning the rules
of the road and the principle of the internal combustion
engine, without finding out how to drive a car in heavy traffic
or on motorways and freeways. This book puts you in the
driving seat of the language, so that it takes you where you
want to go.

Words in a dictionary are like objects in a museum: they
are interesting but merely on display. When words are used
in communication, they come to life and go to work for us.
In this book you see what happens when words are in action
in all the different ways of communicating, from letters to
advertising, on television and radio, in sermons, when speaking
to your wife, your husband, the person you work for or the
people who work for you. You will see how to link ideas and
principles to build up an understanding of how to use words
to deliver the results you want. For whatever form it takes,
communication that works brilliantly uses, consciously or
unconsciously, the same principles. By seeing how these principles operate in different media and in many different situations,
we can learn to understand them and use them for ourselves.

This is not a book about writing good English in a
grammatical or academic sense. Other people, from Samuel
Johnson and Noah Webster to the Fowler brothers and Eric
Partridge, have already done that for their times, although
books like theirs will continually need to be written. English
is well and living in many different countries, so it is constantly
changing. Every few years we need a checkup on the language,
which is why I wrote a book called *A Guide to Good English in
the 1980s*. By the 1990s that book needs to be rewritten.

At times anyone can feel uncertain about grammar or how
to use or pronounce certain words. After all, Robert Burchfield, chief editor of Oxford English Dictionaries, no less,
admitted there is at least one word he pronounces differently
every time he says it. Too often doubts about usage derive
from an old-fashioned belief in rigid fixed rules, because there
are hardliners who believe that teaching English is teaching
dos and *don'ts*. Such fetters cannot be clamped on to a language
as free and volatile as ours. The chapter in this book called
Good and bad English blows away a lot of old cobwebs and
offers guidelines on how to adapt to changes in the use of

English now and in the future.

But in no way is this a textbook. It is written using the insight and ideas of many people who are confronted every day in their work and lives by the pressures to use words to get results (see the list of contributors at the end of the book). Its aim is to help everyone to make their way against the odds, because the odds are usually put up by other people whom we have to convince and persuade before we can move on. Most of us need this help one way or another, whether we are university graduates or started careers straight from school. A large vocabulary is no guarantee that anyone can use words successfully and can even get in the way. Even government departments are getting that message and dreary old circumlocutions such as 'Unemployment Exchanges' are giving way to the simple immediacy of *Job Centres*.

If you want words to do what you want them to, the first step is to understand how communication works and how human beings are affected by it. So in this book you will find the experience of people who are outstandingly successful at using words to deliver the goods. You will meet some of the top advertising people in the world, chairmen and presidents of companies, successful writers, famous broadcasters, Members of Parliament, US Senators, even bishops and millionaire songwriters. Some of them seem to have a magic touch when it comes to putting across a message and you will find here the best advice they can give.

For the first time, secrets and advanced techniques of advertising are applied to our ordinary day-to-day problems of using words in any situation. Because according to Marshall McLuhan, who had revolutionary ideas about media and communication, 'historians will find that the ads of our time reflect the range of activities'. Top copywriters in big London or New York advertising agencies can get paid £60,000 or $100,000 a year plus a whole lot of other benefits. Over a year copywriters do not write all that many words, not nearly as many as journalists, but they know how to use words to attract, to convince and to sell. We find out what we can learn from them.

Nor is it guesswork. Too much is at stake. Research companies are employed to test copy, to see whether the ideas come across, TV commercials are screened in front of sample audiences, and probed for factual communication and psychological impact. Add to that the vital test: is the product selling and are the words getting results? In these ways we learn what works and what does not work. We learn that the difference between knowing how to use words and just 'having a go' can make a difference of millions of pounds to companies, can affect the fortunes of individuals, the success of causes and even the way of the world.

We do not have to believe that the values and attitudes of our society always relate to the pursuit of happiness. That is something else. But if we live in the world, then we need to know how to survive in it; knowing how to communicate effectively is right in the front line. Heads of state everywhere are realising this: Joe Grimond, former leader of the Liberal Party in Britain, comments wryly that 'Advertising in the bureaucratic mind is the key to success, the solver of all problems.' But whether we like it or not, a government in a democracy cannot survive without getting its messages across.

It is the same for you and for me, which is why you can call this book a survival kit. To be successful, or even just to get by, generally requires us to be able to influence other people at times. We must use words for our own good, or to help someone, or for a cause we believe in, or for the good of our country, or the good of mankind. Whatever the reason, the pages that follow are aimed at helping you to get through to people. The advice is meant to be warm and friendly and the ideas easy to take in. It requires so much effort to overcome the anxieties and difficulties of life and there is no need to add to that here.

Most of the ideas are simple. They are taken from the direct experience of people who are outstanding at using words to get results and all the examples come from real life. Everything you will read here has been thoroughly tested in the most demanding of all laboratories: the marketplace of goods, ideas, proposals and causes.

The Superlanguage

English is the superlanguage because it gets through to more people in more countries than any other language in the world.

No one can work out how many people in the world use English as part of their daily lives and even if they did the figure would soon be out of date. For all the time everywhere millions more people are scrambling to learn the language or pick up enough words for one purpose or another. By the 1990s, it is calculated that English will be the language of 75 per cent of the world's radio and television programmes, 80 per cent of all the world's letters, telexes and fax transmissions and 85 per cent of all the information stored in the world's computers.

So the fact that you can read this book gives you a head start. You know the most valuable language on earth. If you were born in Great Britain, the United States, Australia, Canada, New Zealand, South Africa or in any other country where the English language is your birthright, you are sitting on a fabulous asset. The language you speak without effort is the number one language of our time.

In Paris, Rome, Naples, Tokyo, Hamburg, Stockholm, Tel Aviv and in every other major city, teaching English is big business. A survey in 1988 showed English as the one language that nearly all parents in non-English-speaking countries want their children to learn. Everywhere men and women are working flat out and paying high fees to get a share of the linguistic riches that were dropped straight into your lap. Alan Maley, who has encouraged the teaching of English in his work for the British Council, tells us that in every country where he has worked 'English is worn as a badge of modernity, carried as a passport to well-paid jobs.'

When you know English, the way is open to some of the greatest literature in the world. The miracle of Shakespeare alone takes care of that. He even helped to make the language for us. If you 'have seen better days' and are 'poor but honest'; or 'haven't slept a wink' because someone has 'made you mad'; if something is 'all Greek to you' or simply 'neither here nor there'; when 'there is method in your madness' and 'last but not least', 'to tell the truth and shame the devil', 'your heart's desire' is to 'have a charmed life' and to be 'as sound as a bell', because it is 'cold comfort' to be told 'you can only die once'—you are not only speaking English, you are speaking Shakespeare.

If the God of Literature has only one divine son, it is surely

Shakespeare. And he wrote in English. In our own time, as we nudge the 21st century, some of the best writing in English, even much of it published in England, is being written by writers in other countries. American novelists, South African playwrights, Jamaican poets are all contributing to the literature immediately accessible to all of us who know English.

English offers a greater choice of words than most other languages. In French-English, English-French dictionaries, the English section is thicker. The *Concise Cambridge Italian Dictionary* has three hundred pages for Italian-English but five hundred for English-Italian. English is rich in words because history has made it a linguistic melting-pot. That history is described by the BBC as 'the extraordinary tale of a language that came from nowhere to conquer the world'. For English started life as an obscure dialect brought to England in the 5th century by Germanic tribes. Judging by the many early English place-names in the south of England and the Midlands, these tribes spread across the country, taking their language with them.

In 1066, the best remembered date in English history, came the Norman Conquest, which led to English getting thoroughly mixed with Norman French. The vocabulary took on vast shiploads of words from the mainstream of Romance languages, so that we can now recognise thousands of words in French, Italian, Spanish and other languages descended from Latin.

William Caxton and his printing press at Westminster, set up about 1476, took English a step forward, as from then on books could be produced faster and cheaper than manuscripts. A hundred years later and on into the 17th century, English basked and stretched in the warmth and glory of Elizabethan England, making and being made by Shakespeare and the Authorised Version of the Bible.

The 18th century, with its scientific outlook, disciplined and polished English, as it became a language of reason and philosophy, although even then the language extended not much further than Great Britain, two islands on the edge of Europe. The 19th century changed all that, as the imperial expansion of British power carried our language all over the world. English had arrived and in smug Victorian England was settling down complacently, which is the worst thing that can happen to any language or to any human being. But before this hardening of the arteries set in, along came a transfusion of rich vigorous new blood from America, a linguistic lease-lend of young colourful words that has been shaking up the language ever since. More than any other language, English has been kept on its toes and has become the most lively and adaptable language the world has ever known.

All the people all over the world who want to learn English care little about such matters of philological history. For most of them, this is what really counts: English comes first by a long way at doing the very thing for which language came into being—to communicate with other people. No other language is understood by such a diversity of people in so many different countries. So English is the first language for world-wide communication in a crisis, the obvious language for Rajiv Gandhi to choose, when he spoke on television after the assassination of his mother, the Prime Minister of India.

English is the official language of the Olympic Games, wherever they are held, the language of international scientific or economic conferences, the language of flying and shipping—and the obligatory language, or at least a smattering of it, of every waiter, taxi-driver and air hostess. Anybody who wants to be somebody on the international scene must know some English. In the United Nations' buildings in New York and Geneva and in UNESCO in Paris, English is the language you hear most. Any important book written in another language is soon translated into English.

Hungary, Italy, Japan, Mexico, Peru, and on into over half the other countries of the world, are adding to their vocabularies hundreds of English words. In Panama, a puncture is called a *flataya*, in Madrid, you take your clothes to dry cleaners for *el pressing*. As for France, so many English words have taken over that the hybrid language is called *Franglais*. Parisians 'cherchent le *parking* pour faire le *shopping* pour le *weekend*.' Pre-war English-French dictionaries translated 'weekend' as *le bout de la semaine*. Now everyone in France says *le weekend* as well as *le gadget, le cornflakes, le pullover, le marketing, le know-how, le check-up* and *le jogging*.

In Tokyo, *Japlish* has turned someone who works for a business into a *salaryman*. In Germany, not even the Berlin Wall holds back the advance. At an East German bar you can get an orange juice by asking for an *Apfelsinensaft*, if you know the word, but you might as well take it easy and say *Ein Juice*. Record shops in every country sell *singles*, *LPs*, and *CDs*, for there is only one language of pop music and that's English.

English is so successful because it is also the language of the United States. But ask Americans what language they speak and the answer will be *English*. English, the language of Stoke-on-Trent and Stoke Newington, of Old Sodbury and the Old Kent Road, the language of Chelsea Pensioners, Oxford dons, Wiltshire farmers, the Archbishop of Canterbury and the late John Lennon. If it is also the language that Bing Crosby crooned in, the White House declares in, the language you hear on the New York subway, on the Mississippi River, in Silicon Valley, the super-rich information-technology suburb half an hour's drive out of San Francisco, and in so many other expected and unexpected places, from the Australian outback to the road to Katmandu, we can all be grateful for the number and variety of places and people where and by whom we are understood.

English is the superlanguage because it gets through to more people in more countries than any other language in the world.

All we have to do is to use it.

Making words work harder for you

Language is an implement quite as much as an implement of stone and steel . . . it does things to you just as a metal or a machine does things to you.

H. G. Wells, *In Search of Hot Water*

How do you go about writing a letter that a lot depends on?

Do you first decide what you want to say and then write it out in rough? Perhaps you dictate a draft, or even the final version, off the top of your head. If it's a draft, do you then go over it, changing a word here and there, taking this out, putting that in and turning a sentence round so that it sounds better? The chances are you are working within the same habitual pattern of using words and there is no real breakthrough.

You may be losing a great deal, because the words we use play such a big part in our contacts with people and often turn things one way or the other for us. These may not always be real values; but in the rough and tumble of life we cannot help reacting to words that are written and said to us, just as others react to our words. Even in intimate human relationships, we need to find the right words at the right time. Take the banal situation of a man coming home late for dinner, or a women keeping a man waiting. Communication can work— or not work.

The last time John came home late, there was a row. His wife was hungry, the meal spoilt and he hadn't phoned her. Again he lets himself in through the front door and calls out apprehensively 'I'm sorry I'm late darling'. That's exactly what he said last time, so you could hardly expect it to do much good now and produce a relaxed drink, after a hard day in the office or wherever, followed by a quiet friendly dinner later on.

The difference between the way most people use words and the way an athlete works at improving his track record is that the athlete is never satisfied. He knows that by analysing his technique and making changes he can improve his performance. That is the only way to think about words, if you want to be good at using them.

The president of an advertising agency in Los Angeles pitches for new business by asking advertisers if they are satisfied with the results they are getting from their present advertising. If the answer is *no*, the door is wide open for him to talk about moving their account to his agency.

But if the answer is *yes*, he follows up with this question:

Have you ever considered that you might be able to get 50 per cent more results from the same expenditure? At least, it's worth looking at, isn't it?

His agency regularly adds new clients to its list of accounts. And generally they do step up results, sometimes by much more than 50 per cent. One reason is that they take a new look at what had become an old problem. By starting afresh, free from hang-ups over old ideas, they focus more sharply on the *results* they want. Just from that, it often follows that the new advertising is much more successful.

This is the clue to the first step, and it is a very big step, towards making words work harder for you. Shift the focus from 'What do I want to say?' to *What results do I want?* Then you forget about expressing yourself and concentrate on getting through to the other person. The two things are not the same. Every successful copywriter understands that but not everyone else does. This idea is so simple that it is easy to overlook how much it can do for you. It can change your whole approach to every communication you make.

A communication is often an ego-trip. Remember the man coming home late and calling out '*I'm* sorry *I'm* late, darling'. Communications like that say: this is how I feel, this is what I want to say, this is what I want you to do for me, this is how frightened I am. The moment you take all that energy and let it loose on what you want your letter, conversation, interview or telephone call to achieve, things start to happen.

Read this application sent to the personnel manager of a big company:

I am writing in answer to your advertisement for a secretary/assistant to your Export Director.

Your advertisment mentions typing skills, and although I can type accurately and use a wordprocessor, I prefer a position where I do not have to do that *all* the time.

You also say that a knowledge of French would be an advantage. I do know some French, and would be very glad if the job you are offering would help me to improve it.

I have always wanted to work for a company like yours, because I like all the social contacts you can make

in a big organisation. In fact the kind of work I'd really
prefer is a job dealing with people.
Unfortunately, I've already booked up my holidays
for this year. The dates are . . .

And so it went on. The personnel manager said wearily 'The
only thing left out is what she'd like for lunch!'
The writer of that letter did not get on the short list,
although the job might have suited her. She could have asked
about holidays and all the other things at an interview, which
she might well have been offered if she had written:

I can type accurately and am competent with a wordprocessor. But I am also good at dealing with people, so
could bring other things to the job as well. I already
know some French and would want to work hard at
learning more in order to help your Export Director.

It is saying the same thing, but in a very different way.
Even sophisticated organisations can make the same mistake.
Alistair Cooke, the eminent Anglo-American broadcaster, tells
how he was approached by a leading banking corporation
about making a television commercial. On their grand
embossed notepaper, he read:

Congratulations! You have been chosen as the image to
represent our business.

Does that sound like an ego-trip or doesn't it? According to
Mr Cooke, his first impulse was to tell them 'Screw you!' But
he turned them down politely, although they were offering a
million dollars, spread over ten years, in return for what
would have amounted to not much more than a day's work.
Suppose the great banking corporation had directed their
letter simply at the result they wanted, to get Alistair Cooke,
a distinguished celebrity who had never made a commercial
before, to consider their request. They might then have set
about it like this:

We believe that, in the general way, you would not want
to make a television commercial. But some of us here

sincerely feel that you personify the kind of integrity that we try to have as a bank. So we are inviting you to consider making a television commercial for us based on a script that we should, of course, agree word for word with you.

The fee we could offer would be generous. It would amount to $1,000,000, spread over ten years. We should need to take up no more than a day or two of your time.

We all know that money is a temptation although we could well understand that you would not want to be too influenced by it over something like this. It is more important for you to know that our TV commercial will be fair and straightforward.

There may also be causes close to your heart which part of the fee could enable you to support in a way that would not otherwise be possible.

At this stage, would you be prepared to discuss it with us? We'll do our best to satisfy you on any points you want to raise.

We don't know whether that letter would have received an encouraging response from Alistair Cooke but, as the president of the ad agency in LA says, 'At least, it's worth looking at, isn't it?'

This approach introduces into communication the whole concept of *function*. We rate a piece of machinery according to how well it does its job. The simple function of a car is to get us from one place to another safely and economically. When Sir Alec Issigonis' *Mini* first appeared in 1959, it so clearly put function first. The combination of small wheels and the innovatory transverse engine, which took up much less longitudinal space, led to a smaller car, without loss of stability, that could easily nip in and out of town traffic. The result was an overnight and enduring success. In passing, it is interesting to note that the long-lasting successes in the history of the motor car, the Model-T ford, the VW Beetle, the 2-CV Citroen, have all been celebrated for their reliable function and economy.

A car designed to satisfy our egos would not function as well. It may be less economic and even less safe. We are often prepared to accept that trade-off, if we want a car to impress our friends, compensate for a feeling of inadequacy, make us feel young or attract women or men we take a fancy to. We get what we want and pay the price for it.

It is the same with words. We may want to let off steam or assert ourselves and that's all we care about. But if instead our communication has to influence someone, to get people to do something for us or for others, or to accept a point of view, then our words will work much harder if we turn them away from our self-indulgence and point them towards the result we want.

As soon as you analyse the function of a communication, whatever form it takes, you start looking at words in a new way. A communication becomes a piece of machinery and the first question is: Will it work? H. G. Wells, who achieved what he wanted in life through words, said that 'language is an implement quite as much as an implement of stone or steel . . . it does things to you just as a metal or a machine does things to you'. We can borrow that analogy gratefully, as a valuable way to look at any act of purposeful communication.

This is what happens when a letter is aimed simply and accurately at getting results. Like nearly all the examples in this book, what follows actually happened.

Keith invited his girl friend to spend the night in his flat. The next morning, while she was taking a shower, she dropped a heavy glass bottle of toilet water and it cracked the shower tray.

Keith played it cool (what else could he do?) and said it didn't matter at all. But that's not how he felt. The tray was fixed into a recess with quarry tiles cemented in all round. To put in a new tray meant that everything had to be hacked out and replaced. The heavy bottle of toilet water had been a gift from him to her, and that didn't make him feel any better.

The first thing he did was to send in a claim to his insurance company and keep his fingers crossed. After the usual delay, he received the following reply:

Thank you for your letter dated the 17 August, together with the completed claim form.

We have to advise you that this accidental damage

25

does not constitute a claim under the terms and conditions of the Policy, as accidental damage of shower trays is not covered.

When he read the policy carefully, he saw that it listed baths, washbasins, sinks and WC pans, but not a word about shower trays. A phone call to his insurance brokers confirmed that there was a case for rejecting his claim.

He wanted to write to the insurance company calling them a load of sharks, low-lives and con-men. That would have made him feel better, until he got the bill for the repair. The estimate came to £400, $600 or more, a lot to him but nothing much to insurance companies. So he directed every word in his letter towards the result he wanted:

I have received your letter rejecting my claim because you do not consider that the terms of the Policy include accidental damage to shower trays.

I sincerely believe that this is not fair. It looks as if the wording of the Policy goes back a number of years to a time when showers were uncommon. So it doesn't mention them.

You will agree that nowadays many people have showers and that they are not at all exceptional. They are even officially recommended as a way of saving fuel.

Because it seems to me that I am being penalised by an unintentional omission from your Policy, I feel justified in making a complaint of unfair treatment to the British Insurance Association.

You are such an old-established and respected insurance company, that before doing this it seems reasonable to write to you first to see if you will reconsider my claim.

It is all straightforward and quiet. Let us take it apart and see why it works so well.

Keith starts off by quoting their reasons for rejecting his claim. Then he lets them off the hook by suggesting that the wording of the policy may be out of date by chance rather than intention. Next he makes a statement that they have to agree with, which is that showers are common these days. The threat about complaining to the British Insurance Association is to make sure that his letter is passed higher up the line than the claims department, which has to go by the book.

At the end he treats them with respect by asking to have his claim reconsidered. That puts them in a superior position, as they have to 'consider' something. The reply came quickly:

> We are in receipt of your communication dated 7 September.
> We apologise for excluding the shower as of course under present day fittings showers would be covered.
> A cheque for the sum of £400 will follow.

And it did.

Keith is a well known copywriter, so he knew what he was about. It had taken him an hour to write his letter, which makes it his best hourly rate ever—even in advertising. His letter is a well designed instrument of communication, constructed to function efficiently, which it did. It is a good model for any situation when you have to try to get something put right or reconsidered. At first glance it seems a simple letter; but then the *Mini* looked like a simple car.

It is not often that a poet writes for results. Andrew Marvell (1621–78) wrote poetry but as he was also a politician writing newsletters to his constituents and pamphlets attacking the government, he could use words for action. In his private life, Marvell was faced with the problem of what he called his coy mistress, 17th century parlance for a reluctant virgin.

He wrote a love poem to her, but not one full of how *he* felt and what *he* longed for. Instead he designed it step by step, as a means to an end, to persuade his girl to come across. There's no need to give it in full here, because if you are not already familiar with it, you can find it in many anthologies.

Marvell says that if there were all the time in the world, his girl could wait as long as she wants before going to bed with him. But it's not like that; time is never on our side:

> . . . at my back I always hear
> Time's wingéd chariot hurrying near:

And yonder all before us lie
Deserts of vast eternity.
Thy beauty shall no more be found;
Nor, in thy marble vault, shall sound
My echoing song: then worms shall try
That long preserv'd virginity:
And your quaint honour turn to dust;
And into ashes all my lust.

It is quiet and elegant, with courtly 17th century turns of phrase. But the cutting-edge, when it comes, is as sharp as a razor:

The grave's a fine and private place,
But none I think do there embrace.
Now, therefore, while the youthful hue
Sits on thy skin like morning dew,
And while thy willing soul transpires
At every pore with instant fires,
Now let us sport us while we may!

The principles of communication for results have always been the same. Marvell defined what he wanted and never lost sight of it. His poem is a fine example of purposeful writing. Sadly, we shall never know whether it delivered the goods for him, as literary scholars have never bothered to find out. It deserved to work, as well chosen lines from it have worked many times since to help out other men, and also women, caught up in the same predicament.

There is no need to think that writing for results cannot be done with style and humour. It doesn't all have to be push and shove. We can read Marvell's poem for its wit and imaginative use of English, as well as for a lesson in making words work.

When you are writing, you can think as long as you like. But to say the right thing at the right moment, you have to think quickly. If you focus on the result you want, there is a much better chance that the right words will come into your head.

Arthur Pinero's play, *The Second Mrs Tanqueray*, which opened in 1893 at St James's Theatre in London, was revolutionary, a serious play about relationships in a theatre given over to burlesque and melodrama. Pinero was so nervous about how the public would react, that he couldn't bear to watch the first act and instead went for a walk in nearby St James's Park. He came back in time for the interval, and Mrs Patrick Campbell, the actress playing the lead, asked the question actresses have asked down the ages: 'How was I?'

Pinero could have said that he was too worried to watch. That would have been thinking of himself. But he wanted his leading lady to go back on stage for Act Two with confidence. He is said to have replied:

If you can play the second act, my dear, as marvellously as you played Act One, then we shall have the greatest success of all time.

The Second Mrs Tanqueray made a reputation and a lot of money for both of them. The young Bernard Shaw, who was in the first-night audience, said it was the most sensational début of the century.

It is not easy to find just the right words at the moment we need them. It's much easier to think of them as we are going down the stairs on the way out. The telephone can often put us on the spot. We are caught on the hop and cannot think quickly enough. But if you apply the same principle, it will work. Focus on the result you want and do not lose sight of it.

In a small company, production looked as if it were going to be held up by essential parts not coming through. The production manager telephoned the suppliers. They wanted to look into it before they would give him a definite answer. But he knew what he wanted:

Can you find out within an hour? . . .
Say two hours then? . . .
Good. It's now 3 o'clock. I won't budge from my office until 5. Can you call back during that time? . . .
Thank you very much . . . but *before 5 o'clock* please.

Unexpectedly a friend calls you from another country. She is very upset and it is hard to know what to say because there is no time to think. This is a situation we have all been in, when it is so easy to hang up feeling inadequate and flat, because we have not said anything meaningful. You know you want to comfort her, and if you keep that aim in front of you, perhaps the last words you say will be something like 'I'll think of you every day'.

The key to making a communication work for you or help someone else is to project the words away from yourself on to the result you want. In this book, this principle comes up time and again because it is a psychological truth that a new insight must be repeated many times before it becomes part of us.

In big advertising agencies all over the world there are men and women who can evaluate words in relation to overall marketing plans and objectives. If they are good at their job, they focus clearly on the result the advertising has to achieve. When advertising fails, it is often because results have taken second place to something else. At creative meetings, copywriters and art directors are sometimes carried away by their own ideas. They are off on an ego-trip and if they take everyone else along with them, the advertising, brilliant and beautiful though it may be, can be wasteful or a complete disaster.

The best advertising comes when creative originality is harnessed to a clear purpose. Some of the most depressing advertising is the result of self-indulgence. When we study advertising, it helps us to be more objective in our own use of words.

Notice when you are stopped by an advertisement and start to read it. If it has made you interested in the product advertised, it is working for results. Look at it again to see how it works. If it has simply made you interested for a moment in the advertisement, rather than in the product, it is more likely to be a misguided ego-trip than a good piece of communication machinery. Look at that too, to avoid making the same mistake.

To see advertising with no frills but simply directed towards results, turn to the pages in your newspaper given over to small mail-order ads. It has been said that the best test of a copywriter is writing mail-order ads. The cost per reply and the cost per sale are usually worked out exactly. If the same advertisement appears week after week, you can be sure it works. Mail-order ads are often crude and simplistic but they reveal the bare bones of communication.

I have seen late-night television shows in Chicago with commercials given 'live' by a secondhand-car salesman. The salesman stands beside the car, talks about it, says how much and knocks it down to the first person to telephone. Communication stripped for action! When you look at other TV commercials, try to see how they are working, or whether they are working at all. Self-indulgence can be very expensive when even fifteen seconds 'on the box' costs thousands of pounds.

We may not want to descend to the blatant hard sell of secondhand-car salesmen, but all communication has to be disciplined if it is to function well. Sir Arthur Quiller-Couch, a Cornishman who became the first Professor of English at Cambridge, was one of Alistair Cooke's tutors at that university. Cooke has described an essay he had written, the third page of which 'was possibly the most brilliant piece of prose ever written by a Cambridge undergraduate'. Quiller-Couch looked at the essay, shook his head over the third page, and said: 'Cooke, you must learn to *murder your darlings*'. He meant: be ruthless with ideas or phrases you fall in love with. They can turn your communication into an ego-trip.

One of the best aimed TV commercials was made by Groucho Marx, now making more laughter in heaven. Marx's son, Arthur, had written Groucho's biography. Like a good father, Groucho was promoting the book on television in New York with a series of five-second spots. There seemed to be only one of these short commericals, which was repeated time and time again, but no one ever tired of watching it.

Groucho rolled his eyes, stopped chewing his cigar for a moment, and said: 'I hear my son's written my biography. I'd better get outa town—quick!' And he was gone.

That was communication with economy, accuracy and right on target. It made you interested, told you what the book was about and made you want to read it . . . not bad in five seconds flat!

Whenever you are vague or disorganised about the result

you want, you are taking a big chance on what happens to your letter, report, telephone call, or at a meeting. Words can be successful only when they are directed towards a clearly defined end. It is invaluable advice to crystallise the results you want; crystals are always sharp and defined, with clear-cut facets. That is the perfect way to visualise the results you need from any important communication in any form.

Listen for a moment to how Sir Winston Churchill applied this principle. It is May 1940. Neville Chamberlain has just resigned and Churchill has formed a new war-time adminis-tration. He rises to his feet to address the House of Commons, for the first time as Prime Minister. It is a moment of truth:

You ask What is our aim? I can answer in one word: *Victory*. Victory at all costs, victory in spite of all terror, victory, however long and hard the road may be.

That is crystal clear.

Another politician makes a speech. His aim is to win the election and he knows that his best chance is to go after uncommitted voters, because they can be moved one way or the other. This is the beginning of crystallisation and if he works on it, he will get somewhere. What happens instead? It is lonely standing up there in front of a lot of people, so he talks to his friends, the people who are going to vote for him anyway. He gets a standing ovation, comes away pleased but probably without gaining a single extra vote.

The woman who wrote the letter quoted earlier, applying for the job with the export director of a big company, was genuinely interested. Her aim should have been to get an interview, because that was the first step, and every word of her letter should have been directed towards it.

It is important not to ask a communication to do too much at one go, or we could lose everything. The imaginary letter from the banking corporation to Alistair Cooke was not aimed at getting him to agree to make a television commercial, at least not right away. The first step was to get him to consider it: 'At this stage, would you be prepared to discuss it with us?' There is a world of difference between a closed door and one that is kept open.

The man with the broken shower tray did not demand a

cheque from the insurance company. He merely asked them to reopen the file, which would give him the chance to negotiate with them. It was a bonus when they paid up in full right away.

When we simplify what we are asking for, it is easier for people to respond. Some of the best advertisements ask only one thing from the reader. On 2 November 1976, readers of *The Times* were stopped by a whole page that was blank, except for a date written in giant letters:

2ND

NOV.

1992

Below was one short sentence and you can be sure that everyone read it:

> Just a small reminder that, according to statistics, anyone buying a new Volvo today will probably have to replace it on the above date.

There are other reasons why Volvos are good cars but whoever wrote that advertisement picked out a single reason. The result was that every reader of *The Times* that day took in that a Volvo lasts a long time.

Twelve years later, Ford used the same technique. On the 8 August 1988, readers of *The Independent* were stopped by a whole page that looked as if it had been torn off a page-a-day calendar. In large type, it carried the date:

AUGUST

15

MONDAY

Scrawled across it, as if with a felt pen, was the reminder: 'Ford prices go up'. A three-word baseline made the point:

BEAT THE DEADLINE

A whole page ad costs a lot of money and it takes discipline and clear-sightedness to say only one thing in as few words as possible. Both the Volvo and the Ford ads could have said a lot more and people would have come away with a lot less.

Even when we have to say *no* to someone, it is worth thinking through what we want our communication to achieve. Of course we have to make it crystal clear that whoever it is has not got the job, is not going to borrow money from us, get the contract, or stay for the weekend. But if we use our words to help them accept our decision with goodwill, we might make a friend instead of an enemy. Justifying ourselves doesn't help someone else and is usually another kind of ego-trip.

Susan Barton applied for a job as secretary to a TV producer. She was asked to go for an interview and did well at the tests. A month went by and she heard nothing, so she wrote to ask if she had got the job. Back came the reply:

Secretary to Television Producer
We are writing to inform you that you have not been selected for the above appointment.

That was all. The case for writing a more friendly letter is that kindness and consideration were called for in this situation, rather than a slap in the face. There was another reason as well, one they didn't know about: Susan's father was a shareholder in the television company. He wrote an angry letter to the chief executive.

The letter from the insurance company to the copywriter about the broken shower tray didn't do them any good. It just said *no*. If they had directed their letter in another way, he might have accepted their decision.

The next letter from a celebrated publisher rejects a novel but leaves the writer (who in this case happens to be me) almost feeling good about it:

I hope you don't think we have kept your novel an unconscionable time but we have been considering it seriously as it deserves. You convey the horrors of living in a corrupt society convincingly and I found the sexual sequences both unembarrassing and strong.

However, the guy has zero lovability which is bad for business. I just don't see how we could sell enough copies in these hardening times to get by, but I really mean that the book being so well written could be publishable elsewhere.

I am sorry to end with an inelegant sentence so unlike your own.

In a very different situation, a girl wrote this warm and tender letter of rejection:

Dear Bill,
   I cannot marry you. Yet I am so moved by your asking me. If this makes you unhappy, as it might do, please forgive me. It is a consolation for me to know that my refusing you now will one day bring so much happiness to another girl, and that will be the girl you do marry.

There are always rewards for yourself, and sometimes you help others as well, when you clarify your ideas about the results you want your words to achieve and direct them towards that end. A good tennis player does more than send the ball back across the net. He tries to make it land in the right place. 'The difficulty', said Robert Louis Stevenson, 'is not to affect your reader, but to affect him precisely as you wish.'

It is hard work to write a letter that gets just the right result, so it is useful to build up a file of good letters. You can often adapt a letter, use part of it, or let it spark off another idea for any new situation.

We'll go on in the next chapter to look at what it is like for the people at the receiving end, who open our letters, read our telefaxes, answer our telephone calls or sit opposite us at an interview. Before that there is one loose end that was left dangling.

Remember the man coming home late for dinner and faced with a miserable evening? There is no one solution to any problem of communication but we learn from good examples how to find the best way for ourselves. In that spirit, here is the true account of a woman who kept her husband waiting two hours for dinner.

As she let herself in through the front door, she decided that the best thing would be to see it from his point of view, rather than complain about the tedious journey she'd had and the traffic jams. She went straight into him and said 'You must be starving! And it's all my fault.' He agreed with her, admittedly with a *hrrumph*, and poured out a couple of drinks.

Good communication is like good love-making

Every communication, even about the most ordinary things, is an opportunity to throw a bridge across the void.

There is a simple principle that can double the effectiveness of everything you write. One of the highest paid copywriters in the history of advertising said it makes one dollar do the work of ten. It functions not only in advertising and in letters, but at meetings, interviews, conversations and even on the telephone. You can apply it every time you write or say things you hope will do something for you or help someone else.

I heard of it in Chicago, in the office of the head of an advertising agency. His name was Fairfax Cone and the business he built up is now worldwide. That day in Chicago, a writer came in with some copy he had written. Fax, as the boss was called, read it, looked up and asked 'Would you say that to someone you know?' It was an invaluable lesson in communication.

So much of what we write is to people we have never met. The millions who read advertisements are complete strangers to the people who write them. On the telephone, we often speak to people we don't know and will never meet. If we write or speak as if those people are strangers, how can they respond to us? Fear of strangers, xenophobia, is a basic fear of mankind and when we are afraid of something we back away from it.

The first principle of good communication is to treat the other person as a neighbour. Look them in the eye, in your imagination, and make real contact with them as sharing our human situation. That situation is essentially lonely. Every communication, even about the most ordinary of things, is an opportunity to throw a bridge across the void. Then our letters, conversations, speeches and phone calls have more effect than we could ever have believed possible.

Douglas Hurd, who has wide experience of politics in Britain, as political secretary to Edward Heath when he was prime minster, and as a cabinet minister in Margaret Thatcher's government, says that top politicians must always ask 'How would I explain that if I were sitting in the living-room of one of my constituents?' Peter Hobden, a London copywriter, wants his copy to 'feel warm and comfortable'. Jane Ellen Murray, a creative director in Chicago, thinks of the advertisements she is writing as people. 'Would you invite it over to dinner?' she asks and even 'Would your daughter want to marry this ad?'

Some of that may sound far-fetched, but see what happens when this principle is ignored. Here are three letters, the first from a bank manager:

> After your visit here, we considered your request, and regret that, in the light of the securities you are able to provide, we are unable at the present time to agree to the overdraft facilities that you require.

Would you say that to a friend? The woman who received the letter moved her account to another bank. The second letter is from a driver to the police:

> An officious busybody of a traffic warden gave me the enclosed parking ticket. She didn't even stop to ask whether I had a good reason for leaving my car parked on double yellow lines. Oh no! She was too busy writing out more parking tickets.

Would you say that to a friend? The driver had to pay the penalty. A third letter is from a woman to her dentist:

> I have received your account and am enclosing a cheque for half your charges, which is all I intend to pay. The work you did on my two teeth was no good at all. I was in a lot of pain afterwards, and because you were away on holiday, I had to go to another dentist.

Would you say that to a friend? The patient had to pay the fees in full.

Here are those three letters again, but now rewritten as one human being talking to another. From the bank manager:

> I enjoyed meeting you and have thought a lot about your request for a loan. Unfortunately, we cannot do it for you, at least not on the basis of the securities you can offer. I'm very sorry, because I know how much it means to you.
>   Is there any possibility that you can offer better

security, such as a personal guarantee from a friend?

You are always welcome to come back here and talk about any ways we can help you. I'll do my best.

There is a good chance the bank would have kept the customer.
From the driver:

Can you please help me? There wasn't time to explain to the traffic warden, who gave me the enclosed parking ticket, why my car had been left on double yellow lines. So may I tell you how it happened and hope you will consider cancelling the penalty?

He might have got off, if there were good reasons for leaving the car there. From the dentist's patient:

Thank you for your account. I'm so sorry to have to tell you that I had a lot of pain after the fillings, although I know you did your best for me. It was bad luck, because of course I wanted to come back and ask you to look at my teeth. But you were on holiday and all I could do was go to another dentist.

Neither of us could help this, so would you be willing to accept the enclosed cheque for half your fees? As you know now, I have to pay the other dentist as well.

I hope you had a good holiday.

That might have been the end of the matter.

As in those letters, there is often a conflict of interest: you want one thing and the other person wants something else. Suppose your secretary has a date and is anxious to get away on time. But you want her to stay on to get a letter out. If you can help her to identify herself with the situation you are in, there might be goodwill all round. It could go like this: the letter is to an important customer . . . if we don't fax it this afternoon we could lose the business . . . will you help us to keep it?

A successful order always helps the other person to become identified with the purpose of it. We cannot be all things to all people but if we take the time to imagine what it is like to be the other person, they will often meet us half way. Otherwise our communication, whatever form it takes, stands much less chance of getting results—unless we tote a gun.

In *Damn Yankees*, an old musical about baseball, there was a song that always had encores, because audiences responded to it. It had the refrain that, no matter how good a player you are, *You've gotta have heart!* It's the same with communication. The word *heart* often comes up in advice about getting through to people. Sir Arthur Quiller-Couch, the professor of English at Cambridge, said 'Good style consists of thinking with the heart as well as the head'. Henri Cartier-Bresson says the art of photography, another form of communication, is 'putting one's head, one's eye and one's heart on the same axis'.

That master of communication, Alistair Cooke, tells how he finds himself talking to his typewriter, because he is aiming at 'the perfect conversational tone of one man talking to another'. For Jane Austen, writing letters was like 'talking almost as fast as I could'. It is in fact a good idea to talk aloud our letters, or anything else we write, and listen to see if we are keeping the reader at arm's length, or are we friendly and welcoming, as one human being talking to another?

The chief executive of a big international organisation does this, when he writes a letter that a lot depends on: he seals it up in an envelope and gets on with something else. After an hour or so, he slits open the envelope and reads the letter. This helps him to feel what it will be like at the receiving end.

Every so often the senior copywriter in an ad agency on Madison Avenue spends the morning in a supermarket, looking at the faces of the customers and talking to some of them. He says this is the only way he can get the feeling of what it is like to read ads instead of just writing them. Another copywriter worked as a barman for a week in Milwaukee, before settling down to write advertisements for a new lager. Then there's the advertising agency that avoids what it calls the 'ivory-tower disease' by bringing small groups of agency people and consumers together for group discussions.

Jimmy Carter, during his presidency, managed to bring together the President of Egypt at the time and the Prime Minster of Israel for a meeting at Camp David, by sidestepping the Department of State and writing a letter by hand, as from one man to another.

It is easy to forget that every letter we write is read by a person, just as it is always a person who answers whenever we dial a number (answering machines are only a stopgap). Whether you are writing to ICI, Dupont, the Bank of England or the Coca-Cola Corporation, your letter will be read by one person at a time; and it is often the say-so of the first person to read it that decides what will happen next.

Good communication is like good love-making, because both usually involve us with one other person and the more we are aware of that person, the more they will respond.

A TV commercial for a tomato paste showed an Italian newly married to a Polish blond from Cleveland, Ohio. The first time his whole family comes to dinner, of all things she makes an Italian dish—*chicken caccetori!* What can a Polish girl from Cleveland know about Italian cooking?

They are all there waiting: Uncle Giuseppe, Aunt Rosa, Cousin Paulo, Mama, Papa. They give a mama-mia!-what-kind-of-food-is-this? look at the big serving-dish, as the terri-fied young wife puts it on the table. But as soon as they taste it, everyone relaxes: the food is great—just like mama makes! *His* mama of course.

The commercial ends: 'You don't have to be Italian to cook like one. Not when you've got Hunt's tomato paste!' It gets through to us because we are involved.

Big organisations are finding out that it is good business to be personal in their dealings with their customers, and when we see how they do it, we get more lessons in how to make contact with the other person.

At one time, British Airways in New York used the genial actor Robert Morley as their spokesman. He chatted to TV viewers as if they were friends. 'British Airways is expecting you', he announced in 1975, 'for the 200th anniversary of your Revolution. So do come home. All is forgiven!' If you were kept waiting on the telephone, Robert Morley's voice would tell you that he's sorry, but can you be patient for just a bit and they'll be right with you. If you're still waiting a couple of minutes later, back he comes:

Still there, are you? Bravo! I wish I could give you a

prize for endurance. Very soon now I am sure you are going to get your reservation call—*and* have a lovely time.

When he was president of Eastern Airlines, Frank Borman, the former astronaut, did his own TV commercials, so that he could talk to passengers. 'An Eastern plane is late', he said, 'and that really bothers me . . . We'll accept good reasons for being late—but not bad ones . . . And neither will you. So most of the time we'll be on time.' Eastern Airlines' passengers felt involved.

From million-dollar advertising campaigns we come back across the Atlantic to a young photographer who is promoting her one-woman show of photographs in Cambridge, England. She wants publishers and critics from London to come to the private view. The first draft of her letter began:

> I am enclosing an invitation to the Private View of my exhibition in Cambridge, and hope you might be able to attend.

Then she had second thoughts. Cambridge is about sixty miles from London and she was asking people to turn out on a cold and misty November evening. So she tried again, putting herself in the place of the person receiving her letter:

> I know Cambridge is nearly an hour and a half from London and that November evenings aren't inviting. But full of hope, I'm sending you an invitation to the Private View of my exhibition on Thursday, 3rd November. Please try to come.
>
> We'd make you very welcome and there will of course be drinks on hand as soon as you arrive.

By admitting that she was asking people to put themselves out, she won sympathy and a good attendance at the opening of her show.

The secretary of the Writers' Guild of Great Britain did the same thing when she asked members to complete a long questionnaire:

I know you are very busy and that filling in forms is not the most attractive way to spend time, but if you could find time to give us your views the Committee and I would very much appreciate it.

Many of the members of the Writers' Guild, including me, responded. When you see something as someone else will see it, you have gone towards them and are nearer to shaking hands.

An older woman decided, after bringing up her family, to take a training course in order to go back to work again. She is intelligent and has a lot to offer an employer. She began her letter of application:

By the end of this month, I shall have completed a comprehensive business and commercial course at a College of Further Education. This full-time course has covered accountancy, commerce, secretarial duties and typewriting, including some audio and word processing experience.

She sent out twenty letters but none led to an interview. A friend, who is in business himself, suggested that she considered what it is like to be the director or personnel manager who would read her letter. When she had worked up some sympathy for someone in that situation, she wrote another letter, which began:

Can you use in your business a woman who will be loyal, hardworking and reliable? I think I can offer you those qualities and also really up-to-date training, because I am just finishing a comprehensive business and commercial course at a College of Further Education.

Her next six letters led to four interviews.

Even when we are just explaining something, it helps to put ourselves in the other person's place, because it is one thing to have something in our own mind and something different to get it into someone else's. You know what happens when you open the car window and ask the way. You can be treated to a torrent of second turnings on the left, third lots of traffic lights and turn rights at T-junctions. 'Thank you very much.' you say. And the moment he's gone, you turn to your passenger and ask 'What did he say?' Whoever was telling you the way did not put themself in the position of a 'stranger in those parts'.

Seeing things only our way produces breakdowns in communication even at the highest level. Professor A. H. Halsey, the Oxford sociologist, tells us that international conferences are often farces of misunderstanding. When we fail to get a message across, it is a failure of our imagination. Bernard Williams, professor of philosophy at Berkeley, the University of California, is interested in linguistic philosophy. He warns us:

> We have a responsibility to make our words express what we mean, because we do not have these meanings inside us, independent of what we say. Our sentences *are* our meanings.

That is to say, perhaps it is safer to do our best to say what we mean, rather than mean what we say. The difference may be subtle but it is often the difference between a message getting across clearly or being fogbound in misunderstandings. Unless we try to see things as the other person will see them, the shutters will come down and instead of communicating, we end up talking to ourselves.

On a hot summer's day, somewhere in England on a village cricket green, an enthusiastic schoolboy explains the rules of cricket to an American who has never seen the game before:

> One side is out in the field—the other side is in. Each man on the side that's in goes out and when he is out he comes in and the next man goes in until he's out.
>
> When they are all out, the side that's been out in the field comes in and the side that's been in goes out—and tries to get out those coming in.
>
> Is that quite clear, Sir?

As you approach Hemel Hempstead in Hertfordshire, there is

a long steep hill with a big roundabout at the bottom. This roundabout is *two-way* and you can turn either left or right. Most drivers have not met one like it before. When it was first set up like that, there was a sign saying:

EXPERIMENTAL
ROUNDABOUT
AHEAD

There was no explanation and as they reached it, driver after driver goggled in disbelief and dismay at seeing traffic criss-crossing in both directions. People who go that way regularly are used to it by now, but at the beginning, nobody had considered what it was like to be a driver, who expects roundabouts to be one-way systems, unexpectedly coming across a two-way flow.

Even traffic signs can pass on information as if from one human being to another, as one did in Sydney, Australia, when a two-way road was changed to one-way. Any driver who didn't notice saw this sign:

GO BACK
you are going the
WRONG WAY

Carl Gustav Jung, the Swiss psychologist, has taught us more about ourselves than possibly anyone else this century. But his books and papers are considered too difficult to follow for the general reader. Not long before his death, Jung agreed to edit a book explaining his theories to people who have not previously studied psychology. Because he knew this would be difficult, he made it a condition that John Freeman, who had been British ambassador in Washington for a short time and who had interviewed Jung for a television programme, should be the co-ordinating editor of the book.

John Freeman tells how he was rather flattered when the great man chose him, but adds disarmingly that he didn't feel so pleased when he found that it was because Jung thought of him as being of reasonable but not exceptional intelligence, believing that anything John Freeman could understand could also be understood by the average reader.

Jung's approach worked and his book, *Man and his Symbols*, introduced his teachings to many people.

We often have to consider how other people might understand something and the speed at which they can take it in.

If you are a doctor talking to other doctors about the digestive tract, you can go along at a fair gallop. To explain the same thing to an anxious patient, you have to break it down into easily understood facts.

It is a common mistake to transmit information too quickly; we are often afraid of boring people if we slow down. Yet we know from our own experience how quickly we lose interest when we cannot follow something. Next time you hear a speaker going too fast, look at the faces of the people around you and you will see their attention slipping away. With a good speaker, notice his pace and rhythm and how he speaks slowly enough and clearly enough, in short cohesive phrases that everyone can take in without having to work too hard.

That's a good approach to using the telephone, which even now can occasionally feel a strangely uneasy means of communication. It is intimate, because someone is speaking right into our ear and we are doing the same to them: it is also distant, because they are not there beside us. Although most of us are used to it, we often hang up at times feeling we have not said what we wanted, in the way that we wanted to.

After all, when we telephone someone, we do not know and cannot see what state or situation they are in at that moment. They might be in the middle of making love, for all we know, as they reach over to pick up the phone, or doing something equally absorbing, just supposing there is anything equally absorbing. Nor can you always tell from their voice!

Now that telephones are mobile there are even more distractions coming between us and whoever it is at the other end. Walk through any big city, London, Paris, New York, Tokyo, and you will see men and women speaking on their car phones, as they wait in traffic jams, negotiate roundabouts, put their flickers out to turn left or right. We may be speaking directly to someone on the phone but we should never assume that we have their undivided attention.

The telephone is partly replacing direct mail and has almost replaced the old door-to-door salesmen. It is used more and more now as a sales tool because of the high cost of personal selling. There is a girl in New York who has to phone about fifty people every evening, on behalf of a dancing school, and offer them a free dancing lesson. To begin with, every time

48

she heard the *burr* . . . *burr* of the buzzer, she would tense up because she was afraid of being snubbed.

Then she tried propping up by the phone a photograph of a man and woman she knows well. As she looks at it, she finds her conversation flows more easily and her voice is more relaxed. This used to be taught to the first radio broadcasters to give them the feeling of person to person contact.

There is no need to use a photograph, although it helps much more than you might imagine. Another way, when you are phoning someone you know, is to flash into your mind a mental picture of them talking back to you. If it's a stranger, think of someone you like and use a mental image of them. Once you have got into the habit of doing this, you will be surprised at how much it helps you to be more natural and effective on the telephone.

Listen to this conversation that was recorded, for research purposes, on a busy switchboard:

Operator	International Marketing Services.
Caller	Give me Mr Cox, will you?
Operator	Do you know his extension, Sir?
Caller	It's *your* job to know that.
Operator	We've got over five hundred extensions here.
Caller	I can't help that. Just look it up.
Operator	Just a moment then.
Caller	Look operator, I'm in a hurry.
Operator	I'm doing by best, Sir.

A few seconds later.

Operator	He's not answering.
Caller	Well give him a message for me.
Operator	We're not allowed to take messages, Sir. I'll give you another extension.
Caller	I don't want another extension. I want you to give him a message.

At that point the operator pulled out the plug.

Luckily we do not all speak to telephone operators like that, or nobody would get through to anybody. Even on the telephone, maybe especially on the telephone, our words work better when we talk as one human being making contact with another.

What is called the 'passive voice' is considered bad for communication, because it is impersonal. It is the passive voice when you turn sentences round and say 'Your order has been received' instead of 'We've received your order'. Or 'Every attempt should be made by you . . .' instead of 'You should do your best'. Or 'The information you requested has been ascertained' instead of 'We have found out what you want to know'.

'It is felt', 'it is regretted', 'it is appreciated' and so on all have the effect of the passive voice. So-called 'white paper blindness' can lead us into this—we are blind to the other person. As we turn our thoughts round in that way, we may drive a wedge between us and whoever is reading our letters or reports. When we are talking to a friend, we use 'I' and 'you' all the time. 'It' is for objects and not for people. 'You are loved by me' does not sound the same as *I love you*. Jung said, words 'gain life and meaning only when you take into account their relationship to the living individual'.

Mervyn Stockwood, who was Bishop of Southwark, agrees with that. When he was vicar in a tough district of Bristol, he was looking through a draft of his curate's sermon. 'What would this mean to Charlie Hodder?' he boomed out. Charlie Hodder, he explained, weighed about twenty stone, worked on the railways and 'had two places of worship: the church and the pub'.

In some ways, you can think of communication as speaking on the telephone, when it's a bad line, and you have to get through all the crackles and splutters. It is so often like that when we are talking or writing to someone. We have to do our best to get through all the fears, doubts, uncertainties and hang-ups that come between us and the other person.

No matter how clever we are at using words and stringing them into sentences, that is not enough on its own. Then what else do you need? *You've gotta have heart!*

Getting attention first

Instead of showing a big picture of the car you show a big picture of
Marilyn Monroe and a little picture of the car. If that doesn't work,
you take some clothes off her!

Martin Mayer, Madison Avenue, USA

For thousands of years fables have been used to teach unchanging truths about human nature. Here is a fable about communication. The vital truth it contains can help us every time we use words.

It started as an old Russian story with a moral. A century or so later it surfaced again as a cautionary tale told by Rosser Reeves, one of the legendary American admen. The truth behind it is universal and timeless and it could have been told anywhere at any time.

In a remote region of eastern Russia, there was a travelling wizard who could work wonders at training the most difficult of donkeys. All he had to do, it was said, was to talk to the donkey and thenceforth it would obey every order. The wizard went from village to village selling his services.

In one village a peasant had a donkey whose obstinacy knew no bounds. The villagers believed it was a direct descendant of the original stubborn mule. The moment it was loaded up, it would sit down and refuse to respond to threats, beating or cajoling. Even when its owner dangled a carrot in front of its nose, this donkey wouldn't budge. Time and again the peasant had to unload it, curse his luck and carry the stuff on his own back.

When the wizard arrived in that village, you can guess who was the first in the queue. They agreed terms quickly, for the peasant was in no mood to haggle. The wizard began by walking slowly round the animal, examining it carefully. Everyone watched. For if he could make *this* donkey obey orders, then he could truly work wonders. The stranger appeared to be giving the matter considerable thought. Then he made up his mind, rummaged in his bag, took out a large wooden mallet, advanced on the donkey and without hesitation smote it smartly between the eyes.

'I don't want him killed!' protested the owner. 'It's the only donkey I've got and I heard that all you have to do is to talk to him.'

'Then you heard right, my friend' replied the wizard, 'But you must understand something else: I have to get his attention first.'

Has this ever happened to you? You have gone to see your doctor, a lawyer or the boss about something that really matters to you. After a while, you become aware that they

53

have something else on their mind. You see it in the lack of concentration in their eyes and hear it in the mechanical way they ask or answer questions. Most of us have been through this and have come away with a deep sense of dissatisfaction. We could not get across what we wanted to say.

At the same time, we know that when we ourselves are listening to someone, or reading a letter or report, our minds can be full of other things. Try the experiment of stopping and listening to the almost constant chatter going on in your head. Total concentration is so rare that it is said it can work miracles.

If we all gave each other our undivided attention, our responses would be alive and immediate. When we talk to our friends and family, there would be a heightened awareness of one another and every moment would count. But people will not often listen to us or read our words in that way. There are too many things going on inside them. What then can we do about this when it is important to get through to someone?

We can start by raising the level of attention people give to what we are saying or writing. If we lift attention from 20 per cent to 40 per cent, we have doubled it, and that can make all the difference. Let's see this in action. These are examples, again from real life, of the beginnings of letters waiting on a sales manager's desk at 9.30 one Monday morning:

Can we draw your attention to a new scheme for . . .
Our representative would like to call on you to discuss . . .
We understand that you might be interested in . . .
In reply to your letter of 3 July, enquiring about . . .

He goes through the letters quickly, puts some on one side to be dealt with later and drops others into the wpb. In his office nothing stirs. The level of his attention is as flat as the water of a lake on a windless day.

Stifling a yawn, he plods on:

We are in receipt of your letter of 30 August in connection with . . .
If your work involves travelling and entertainment, can

we offer you unique Credit Card facilities? . . .
We have 200 new ideas for putting punch into direct
mail shots and promotion campaigns . . .
Good morning. I'm afraid it could be *Monday* morning.
Just my luck! But that was a chance I had to take. Your
enquiry arrived on Friday and because we would very
much like to have you as a customer, I dealt with it the
same day . . .

Different people are turned on or put off by different things.
The way that last letter began caught the sales manager's
attention. He read it twice and faxed a reply immediately.
When I asked him why, he thought for a moment and said 'I
suppose because it was different. It kinda woke me up a bit.'

Mary Wells Lawrence made a name for herself as chairwoman of a successful advertising agency on Fifth Avenue,
New York and at one time was believed to be the highest
paid woman executive in America. In those days, she said
something very simple about the one thing all her advertisements have in common:

They all shake things up a little bit.
They look at the product or service with a fresh eye.

Whoever wrote the letter that got the sales manager going
that Monday morning had learned to do the same thing. His
letter did not begin in the expected way; it shook things up a
little bit.

When television arrived, everyone thought it was a fantastic
advertising medium. Here at last was the captive audience
advertisers had always longed for. But there was a catch.
Television became known as the *goggle box* as it is so easy to
look at it without any real attention. A *Washington Post* survey
has shown that people watch TV for about twenty-two hours
a week. They also talk at the same time, have their supper,
read the paper and, of course, doze off, all while the TV set
is switched on. One chastened researcher, looking through
findings, said with awe 'When people are watching TV, there
is *nothing* they won't try to do at the same time!' Advertising
people soon found out that unless they get attention in the

first few seconds of a commercial, they are lost.

In the early days of photocopying, a classic commercial began with a chimpanzee loping into an office. Viewers looked up—what's a chimp doing in an office? He was taking a document to the *Xerox* machine and making copies, to show how simple it is. Nearly thirty years later, there are people who still remember that commercial. Thousands and thousands of others are forgotten because they did not lift the level of our attention.

Another successful commercial used suspense. It's a dark foggy night, a woman is driving on her own and she has a flat tyre. Viewers stopped talking and looked. What's going to happen? No problem. She drove on because her Goodyear tyres had built-in safety-spares.

A prize-winning commercial for Phillips screws used involvement. Phillips screws were new at the time, with a cross in the head instead of the usual slot. This needed explanation and viewers would have to pay attention. The commercial started with a man screwing home an ordinary slotted screw. The screwdriver slips and scores a beautifully polished surface. Everyone who has ever driven home a screw was immediately involved. Research showed that viewers looked at and listened to what came next.

The unexpected, suspense and involvement are three effective ways of lifting the level of anyone's attention. Test them for yourself. The moment you see or read something unusual, or a picture or headline connects with your own experience, or something makes you want to know what will happen next, your attention is caught. For the next minute or two you watch the screen or read the paper in a different way. If that happens to you, it also happens to everyone you communicate with.

A woman was getting a divorce. There were many complications and she was confused and worried. She wrote to her solicitor. At the end of the day, he picked out her letter as the one that had stayed most in his mind. This was the first paragraph:

I know this is just one of many cases to you. But it is different for me. It's my divorce and the only one I'll ever have, I hope. My whole future depends upon whether it goes well, so please give me the best advice you can.

'How did that affect you?' I asked him.

'It made me stop and think' he answered. 'It's not the way people usually write to their solicitors.'

'Did it make any difference to how you dealt with her case?' He hesitated. 'I do my best for every client.'

'But?' I asked.

He smiled. 'I didn't say *but*. But . . . ' We both laughed.

'You know how it is' he went on. 'We're all human and whatever you're doing, you can put a little extra into it.'

I said nothing more because it would have been unfair to have pushed the point further. Solicitors, like doctors, surgeons and airline pilots, are supposed to function at peak level all the time. But who can do that? If something unexpected comes in, we sharpen our minds. We should all like to get that kind of attention when we write or say anything in a situation where the response could make a difference to our lives.

Any nutcase can get attention by doing something silly or shocking, or by promising something they cannot deliver. That's not good enough. People walk away when they find they've been tricked into gathering round. Do all those calendars in brash colours, with naked girls in coy poses, do anything more than make garage mechanics from Sidcup to Solihull, New Haven to New Orleans, lust after lovely blondes, brunettes and redheads?

It is fair to add that the famous Pirelli calendars, which started for the year 1964, did succeed in turning a little-known Italian tyre manufacturer into a world-famous name. They startled the whole media world at the time, as the audacity and brilliance of the photography and design made Pirelli calendars privileged collectors' pieces. But even that became too much of a good thing, and after ten years Pirelli got out of it because, it has been suggested, they were becoming better known for calendars than for tyres: the company themselves admitted that they needed to place 'greater emphasis not only on our company name . . . but on the products in the market place'.

After a long gap, Pirelli has resumed publishing their

calendars, but now it is more clearly promotion in line with marketing, and close-ups of the tread of Pirelli tyres are shown. Some of us regret the passing of the spectacular irrelevance of the classic Pirelli calendars, but we can understand the reasons. Getting attention is a top priority in any communication but it should always focus that attention on what is required. When the president of a famous motor manufacturer demanded record attention figures for his ads, the head of the advertising agency replied that was easy enough if nothing else mattered. 'Instead of showing a big picture of the car,' he proposed, 'you show a big picture of Marilyn Monroe and a little picture of the car. If that doesn't work, you take some clothes off her!'

A letter to young executives began:

What could you do with £100,000 hard cash? A new car, your own swimming pool, a long holiday? Why not make out your own list right now?

It did get attention at the start. Then it went on to describe an insurance policy. If you are under thirty and pay so much a month for thirty-five years, that's the sum you might end up with. It was a counter-productive letdown after the opening, which promised something just around the corner, not thirty-five years away.

If you trick people into giving you their attention, there is the risk of a backlash and everything that follows might lose credibility. It is more intelligent to raise the level of someone's attention in a way that relates to what you want to say to them. The man who wrote to the sales manager could have gone too far:

Good morning, I'm afraid that it could be *Monday* morning. And we all know what Monday mornings are like. You have a nice weekend, play golf, see your friends. And then Bang! It's Monday morning again, and here you are driving the car or catching the train to the office. The party's over.

That leads up the wrong alley. The sales manager would have had to read too much and then drag himself back to the point of the letter. As it was, he remembered the letter arrived on Monday because his enquiry had been received on Friday and had been dealt with the same day. He liked that.

In the States clever visual ideas on television, which draw attention away from the product advertised, were called *video vampires*. When, in her heyday, Brigitte Bardot suddenly appeared in a TV commercial for the first time, it was a coup. As you would expect, it wasn't cheap: a Sunday paper at the time said that the whole project cost a fortune.

Brigitte Bardot was not a vampire or even a vamp (the second word is a derivative of the first), but in discussions about the commercial, everyone remembered seeing Bardot looking relaxed and lovely, but not so many people could recall what she was advertising. There is always a risk of a clever idea stealing the show. An experienced politician once warned a new Member of Parliament, who was drafting his maiden speech, 'Don't let the idea upstage the message'.

When you are writing a letter, picking up the phone or going in to talk to someone, remember you have an advantage over all advertisers, even if they have millions to spend. You are communicating with one person. You know their name or can often find it out, you know something about them and can often find out more. Your first sentence can have an immediate relevance for that one person and the relationship between you. Compared to that, no matter how much research advertisers do, they are putting a message in a bottle, hoping that the right person will find it, open it and read it.

I heard a friend make a telephone call to a big department store about a refrigerator that had not been delivered on time. Her old refrigerator had been sold to make space for the new one. It was summer and there was a heat-wave, so she had problems. This was her side of the conversation. She was speaking to the telephone operator to begin with:

> Do you know, or could you find out please, who deals with deliveries to customers in the London area?
> Thank you very much. Do you know his first name? . . .
> And his extension? . . . Thank you. It's really very friendly of you to help me like that. Would you put me through to him please?
> Is that Philip Elliott? . . . Oh good. My name is Mary

Wilcox. I'm so glad to speak to you, because you're the one person who can help me. Isn't it lovely hot weather? I agree. It's marvellous! But would you believe it? I haven't got a refrigerator.

She went on to give him the essential details of her order.
Put that beside the usual approach:

Hallo. Despatch department? I want to make an enquiry about a refrigerator that hasn't been delivered.

My friend started off by finding out the name of the actual man who could help her. She got his attention from the start by showing that she knew his name—'Is that Philip Elliott?' She followed up with the Kitchener-Needs-You approach: 'You're the one person who can help me'. And she went on from there.

I was tempted to go round to the store, find Philip Elliott and ask what effect that phone call had on him. But as it is results that count, I asked my friend to let me know when her refrigerator turned up. She telephoned the next day and invited me round for iced coffee.

When you are trying to think of the best way to capture attention in a letter, at a meeting or in any other communication, it is usually best to look first at the most direct way, even if it seems obvious. Sometimes there is no need to be clever. In 1975 Margaret Thatcher became the leader of the Conservative Party in Great Britain, perhaps the biggest landmark in the history of equality for women since they won the vote in 1928. Soon afterwards, the Conservatives had a political broadcast on television. Political broadcasts are not usually compulsive viewing because people feel they have heard it all before. But here was a real chance to get everyone's attention from the start: there was a star attraction, the first woman in the Western world who was in line to become prime minister.

All it needed was Margaret Thatcher to be there on the screen; she had plenty of experience of television and had been taught how to handle the medium by Gordon Reece, a flamboyant expert on self-presentation. The simple way would have been to open with a close-up of Margaret Thatcher and we'd have been all eyes and ears. What happened instead? The political broadcast began, just as all the others had done, with a man.

Simple beginnings give us a better chance to get to the heart of the matter:

> Good morning. I'm afraid it could be *Monday* morning . . .
> I know this is just one of many cases to you. But it is different for me . . .
> . . . you're the one person who can help me.

Headlines can teach us how to get attention with simplicity and directness. At their worst, they are confusing or you have to think about them. And nobody bothers to do that. When you have to explain a headline, it's like having to explain a joke; it means you have failed. Good headlines say it all in a clear, arresting and memorable way.

Peter Hobden, an experienced advertising writer, was working with a designer on ideas to put over a new breakthrough for London transport. Instead of the tedious journey by bus to Heathrow, London's main airport, passengers could now take an underground train there, all the way from the centre of London. The designer was doodling, the way designers do when they are hunting around for ideas, and he sketched an underground train with the nose of an aircraft at the front. Something clicked and Peter Hobden wrote:

FLY THE TUBE!

The news, the excitement, the speed and the convenience were all there in three short words.

Most pens are shiny. When Parker produced a matt black pen, it looked more distinguished, in the way that the soft sheen of stainless steel looks more distinguished than chromium. The advertising agency had to say that in a few words on a small poster, giving the pen distinction, taking full advantage of the reputation behind the name *Parker* and catching our attention. Their solution was:

ONLY PARKER CAN MAKE A PEN THAT DULL

Here are some other headlines that have stopped people:

WE DON'T THINK PEOPLE SHOULD MAKE
MONEY OUT OF ABORTION

(For a pregnancy advisory service).

WE'RE RICH! JOIN US!

(For a newsletter to help investors).

DON'T GIVE THE GIFT THAT GOES ON GIVING

(For a VD clinic in Berkeley, California).

THE MOST WORTHWHILE WEEKEND OF
YOUR LIFE?

(For a weekend course, at the Manchester Business School, for people who want to start new businesses).

LE CRUNCH—FRENCH GOLDEN DELICIOUS APPLES

(On a barrow of fruit).

Those headlines have one thing in common: they are simple, direct and make a relationship between us and what they are saying.

We cannot always think of a clever idea but we can always start with something simple. This is Sir Richard Steele beginning a letter to his wife, when he was away from home. The date is 30 September 1710:

> I am very sleepy and tired, but could not think of closing my eyes till I had told you I am, dearest creature, your most affectionate and faithful husband.

This is a seventeen-year-old boy answering the first question at an interview:

> No I don't have any experience, sir. I've just left school. But if you give me the job, I'll be as intelligent as I can and work as hard as I can.

This is the beginning of a letter from a woman replying to a final notice to pay an overdue account:

> I will pay the bill. I promise you that. But I can't pay it right away. The reasons don't matter, and would only bore you. Please can I have another month? That's all I need.

Advertising experts say a headline that asks a question is a guaranteed way of attracting attention. It can also work at the beginning of letters, of meetings and even in a poem.

The most arresting first line of any poem was a question by John Donne, the 17th century mystical poet:

What if this present were the world's last night?

When winter was getting under way, this question was at the top of an advertisement:

WHAT WILL YOU DO TOMORROW IF THE CAR WON'T START?

That can also seem like the end of the world. It was an advertisement for an anti-damp spray.

Orbach's is the store in New York that sells women's clothes at lower prices. Some years ago they hooked the attention of every woman by asking:

DOES YOUR BABYSITTER LOOK BETTER COMING IN THAN YOU DO GOING OUT?

A successful letter to local firms used a question as the first sentence:

> Would an experienced, fast and reliable local office cleaning service save you a lot of trouble?

A small company was in an ugly situation because of labour troubles. The managing director went to a meeting with the staff. He began with a question: 'Please can we start off by asking: What is the one thing we all want?' The question made everyone stop and think. If each side wanted something different, there could only be an impasse. But if both sides wanted to get back to work, there was a chance.

If you can make an opening sentence personal, it stands a much better chance of catching someone's interest. The titles of books can sometimes show how. One writer changed 'It Was Always Hot' to *Some Like it Hot*; 'The Witch' became *I Married a Witch*; 'The Lost Wife' was changed to *The Man Who Lost His Wife*.

Instead of starting, as one letter did, 'It is important to have up-to-date information about export markets'. it could have been rewritten 'A chief executive wanted to be right up-to-date about export markets'. That's more involving because it is more personal.

When you use an unexpected approach, you will often be met with 'You can't say things like that'. Don't always listen. Rosie is a copywriter in a big ad agency. Her husband has his own business and she does some letters for him in the evening. She has a lively sense of good communication and often rewrites the beginnings of his letters. In one case, she changed:

> We acknowledge receipt of your first order, but regret that we are unable to deliver by the date specified. The 27 June is the earliest we can manage.

to:

> We were very glad to get your order and welcome you as a new customer. So you can imagine how much we hate saying we cannot make your delivery date. Can you possibly wait until 27 June? If you can, we'll bust a gut to get it to you by then.

'You can't say things like that' her husband said.
'Why not?'
'Because people don't write like that in business letters. That's why.'
'What's so special about a business letter already? It's just one person talking to another.'

With people we are very close to, perhaps especially with those we love, we have to find ways sometimes to lift the level of attention, or a marvellous moment would be lost. Thornton Wilder, the American playwright, captured this in his play *Our Town*. Emily, the daughter of the family, dies in childbirth at twenty-seven. She is allowed back to live one day over again, but she has to watch herself reliving it. She chooses her fourteenth birthday.

As she goes through the morning of that day, she alone knows how little time she has left and she cannot bear the way no one is looking or listening with any real attention. It is all going so fast. She cries out: 'Oh, Mama, just look at me one minute as though you really saw me'.

A father took his twelve-year-old son outside to look at an eclipse of the sun. After a few moments, he clouted the boy round the head. 'I'm sorry, Mike. But I want you to wake up and *look*. Then you'll remember seeing it for the rest of your life.'

Research has shown that people in cities come up against over two thousand advertising messages each day. How anyone works out that kind of figure is not clear, but just accept it. Add the thousands of other impressions made on us from the moment we get out of bed in the morning. Now add to the total those thoughts, feelings, fears and emotions churning around inside us. When we want to get attention from someone—all *that* is the competition.

As long ago as 1710, when life was slower, quieter and simpler, Steele and Addison gave this advice in *The Tatler*: 'The great art in writing advertisements is to catch the reader's eye.' Nearly three hundred years later, every copywriter in every ad agency in every country is still trying to follow that advice. Albert D. Lasker, one of the great masters of American advertising, put it with more punch: 'You must stop the streetcar before you get on it!'

On not boring the pants off them

At the end of a long interview, a tedious reporter asked Abe Burrows what was the low point in his life. Burrows replied, 'I hate to say it, kid, but I think this is.'

Joel Raphaelson, *The Unpublished David Ogilvy*

When we bore someone all communication breaks down. The other person switches off and stops listening or reading. It doesn't matter if it's a friend, our husband, our wife, a customer or the chairman, if we bore them they are no longer with us. From that point on we are wasting our time.

Read this classified advertisement, perhaps the most famous one that has ever been written:

MEN WANTED for Hazardous Journey. Small wages, bitter cold, long months of complete darkness, constant danger, safe return doubtful. Honour and recognition in case of success.

It appeared in London newspapers in the year 1900 and is part of the documentation of Ernest Shackleton's expedition to the South Pole. The words are uninviting and flat; they offer little and promise nothing. Yet the response was overwhelming. Shackleton said 'It seemed as though all the men in Great Britain were determined to accompany me'. What attracted people? In spite of the hardship and the danger, perhaps because of them, the journey must have seemed like an antidote to boredom. And people will do almost anything to escape being bored.

Boredom is like an illness. When we are bored life drags and nothing tastes any good or looks any good. It follows that the last thing we want is to bore someone, because no communication can succeed if it does that. The story is told how, at the end of a long interview, a tedious reporter asked Abe Burrows, the musical comedy writer, what was the low point in his life. Burrows replied 'I hate to say it, kid, but I think this is'.

What happens when you listen to someone talking and it's uninteresting? It can feel like crossing a desert without an oasis in sight. When you read something that doesn't interest you, you don't go on with it, unless you have to. Then it's a struggle and you can imagine you are tired, hungry or even ill, anything that gives you an excuse to stop reading.

Suppose you are the one who is boring someone. How does it feel as the flow of communication peters out? These three situations actually took place:

Case 1

A salesman is with a director of a company, selling him a delivery service for the London area. He talks about the number of messengers they have available on motorbikes, shows him a list of firms who employ them, explains the radio call links and how they are organised.

It is quite impressive. But he comes away saying 'It was no good—he just didn't want to know'. The other man was polite but bored. And that's the death of a salesman.

Case 2

The principal of a New York advertising agency is explaining to the president of a big company the reorganisation of the agency's creative departments.

After a while, the president gets up and says 'I couldn't be less interested in the saga of your company'.

Case 3

A secretary is talking to her boss about her salary. She explains how her fares have gone up, how much she has to pay for lunch and that she is feeling left behind generally in the rates of pay for secretaries.

Her boss looks at his watch and says 'You'll have to excuse me, Sally, but I've got a meeting in a couple of minutes'.

The salesman, the head of the ad agency and Sally all made the same mistake: they did not take into account the limit of interest in the other person. Just as our own time and interest are usually limited, so is everyone else's. The moment we go beyond someone's limit of interest, we start to lose contact. This explains why every year millions of pounds and dollars of communication go down the drain.

Research has shown that if you take a half-page advertisement in a national daily paper, about twenty per cent of readers will not even look at the page; fifty per cent look at the page but not at the advertisement; that leaves thirty per cent who look at the ad, and only some of those read it. Boring people can waste a lot of time and money.

Government departments send out forms with whole pages packed with instructions. The result: millions of forms are filled in wrongly or not filled in at all. 'Life', as the old song goes, 'gets tedious—don't it?'

The way to make any communication in any form alive and interesting to the other person is to keep within their limit of interest or find a way to extend it. Because a limit of interest is not fixed; it always depends upon the involvement of one person with the other or with the subject. When something is about *us*, our limit of interest expands generously. We can extend anyone's limit of interest by turning round what we are saying or writing so that we talk about them. Let's go back on our three case histories:

Case 1

The unsuccessful salesman could have asked 'Do you know how many of your firm's letters are sent to the London area? Generally it's at least 50 per cent. How would you like to be sure that nearly all those letters are delivered the same day at no more cost than first-class postage?'

Case 2

The principal of the New York ad agency would not have bored his client if he had said 'I thought you would like to know we can now put more creative man hours into your advertising without it costing you a cent more'.

Case 3

Sally would have stood a much better chance of getting through if she had said to her boss. 'I know you're under pressure and need all the help you can get. Will you help me to go on doing my best for you?'

The need to talk about ourselves is so strong that it works as a therapy and a wise family doctor knows that just by letting patients talk about themselves, it often does them more good than medicine. When the BBC did a series of radio programmes on psychotherapy, they called it *Let's talk about me*.

At the beginning of her novel, *Persuasion*, Jane Austen describes how Sir Walter Elliot only ever picked up one book, which was the list of Baronets. It always fell open at the same page:

ELLIOT OF KELLYNCH HALL
Walter Elliot, born March 1, 1760, married July 15
1784, Elizabeth, daughter of James Stevenson Esq. of
South Park in the county of Gloucester; by which lady
(who died 1800) he has issue, Elizabeth, born June 1,
1785; Anne, born August 9, 1787; a still-born son,
November 5, 1789; Mary, born November 20, 1791.

All that may take *you* beyond your limit of interest but for Sir
Walter Elliot it was fascinating stuff; he could read it and re-
read it, Jane Austen observed, 'with an interest which never
failed'.

It's like a bad joke in the advertising business when a client
wants to show in his ads a picture of the new factory; and to
tell everyone how big it is, how many people work there and
all the rest of the things he is proud of. The result, for other
people, would be one big yawn.

When, in the early 1960s, Ford in the US was looking for
a name for their new car, more than six thousand were
submitted. Their advertising agency listed *Corsair*, *Ranger* and
Pacer as the top three suggestions. Ford chose *Edsel*, the first
name of Henry Ford I. It didn't mean much to anyone else
and the *Edsel*, for a number of reasons as well as the name,
was the biggest failure in marketing history.

Ruth Waldo, as a group head with J. Walter Thompson,
at the time the biggest ad agency in the world, warned against
copywriters seeing too much of client because 'they begin
thinking about Mr X as the client rather than about the
people who buy the product'.

Whenever we write business letters, sales letters, letters to
help someone; or when we go into a meeting, deliver a Sunday
morning sermon, pick up the phone to speak to a customer or
a friend, it always helps to remember what happens when a
manufacturer shows a picture of his own factory: nobody
wants to know.

This advertisement for a second-hand car appeared in a
local paper:

£700 is dear for a 14-year-old VW Beetle. But it's cheap
if you want the feeling of driving a VW that's done only
25,000 miles and looks *three* years old.

That is interesting because it puts us in the driving seat. Compare it to this letter:

We are glad to tell you about the success of our new car-leasing facilities. In the last year, over 700 cars have been leased through us for the directors and executives of well-known companies. These include . . .

Or this one:

When it comes to office furniture, no one can give you a bigger choice than we can. We have been in the business for fifty years, and we are proud of our Showrooms with their four floors of desks and chairs waiting for you to inspect.
As Managing Director, I should like to add . . .

Those two letters, in their own way, are just showing a picture of the factory.

The surest of all ways to bore people is to write or say too much. We run out of interest the way sand runs through an hourglass. Check your reaction next time a long letter or report lands on your desk or doormat. Most of us recoil from the effort we have to make to get through it. Everyone has too much to read: newspapers and trade magazines pile up, circulars and internal memos plop into in-trays. Put side by side these two letters from women who are replying to a stern letter from their bank manager:

Letter 1
I was horrified to get your letter and to find out the size of my overdraft. The trouble is I had been on holiday on the Costa Brava and had spent much more than I had intended. I'm sure you know what it's like when you go on holiday and just forget how much you are spending.
Then when I got back, my Mini needed new brake linings and one or two other things, so the bill came to £150 which was much more than I could possibly have expected.

73

While I was on holiday, I broke a tooth, and had to have a gold crown fitted and that came to £160 which I'm sure you'll agree is a lot of money to have to find suddenly.

And even that was not the end of it.

Letter 2
Thank you for warning me that I am so much overdrawn. Several emergencies all came together. I'm sorry, because I should have asked you first.
Everything is all right now. I'll be able to clear the overdraft within three months by going carefully.

This was the bank manager's reaction. *Letter 2* gave him confidence in the reliability of his customer and he continued to allow her a modest overdraft.

The length of what we write or say must relate to the reader's or listener's limit of interest or our communication will fall as flat as a pancake. If we are going to buy a new car, we're usually willing to read a lot about it. Specialists have a high limit of interest about any new developments in their field, although remember even experts are sometimes bored out of their minds at conventions and conferences, listening to long papers read by other experts who are carried away by their own knowledge and enthusiasm.

It is, of course, different with literature. If you want to write a novel as long as *War and Peace* (about 600,000 words) go ahead. But you will find that most publishers are much happier with 100,000 words or even less, unless you're a Tolstoy.

It is different also with legal documents where you have to use recognised standard phrases to be as clear and precise as language will allow. This is a special area and length is not so important, although there is the story a young solicitor told against himself. He had gone with his client for a meeting with a busy QC. The barrister opened the meeting by saying that he had time to read only half the brief.

'But that won't do at all!' protested the solicitor. 'All the important matters are covered in the second half.'

'That was the half I read' replied the counsel.

When Johan Gutenburg set up, around 1450, the first printing press using movable type, he started a revolution in communication. For the next five hundred years the printed word was the most effective way of influencing the greatest number of people. Through words in print, revolutions were brought about, governments overturned and social orders challenged. That age has come to an end.

Now elections are won, revolutions are sparked off through television. Ronald Reagan was called the *great communicator* during his presidency, because even though he had been only a run-of-the-mill actor, that experience added so much polish to his presidential appearances on TV. International marketing is increasingly avoiding the problem of different languages by passing on as much information as possible in pictures. The washing instructions on your shirt or skirt and the markings on the knobs and levers of your car are symbols, not words. Nor do you have to read any more to find the right *loo*: an outline figure tells you which door.

We are all used to an electronic immediacy and can get impatient if there are too many words. As we move into the 1990s, David Bernstein, a successful creative consultant in London, warns us 'that the average attention span is down to five seconds and shrinking fast'. We may regret this or not like it, but we must accept that in most day-to-day communications brevity has become vital if we want people to read or listen to us.

Long ago the ancient Greeks believed in this principle and some of the great passages from their literature demonstrate that economy in the use of words can make a passage all the more moving and effective. Plato's comment on the death of his master, which saddened his whole life, was only a few words:

Such was the death of our friend, the best man, I think,
that I have ever known, the wisest too and the most just.

Churchill's economy with words was also inspired and moving. In June 1940 the Germans occupied Paris and soon afterwards the French Government surrendered. Hitler boasted 'The war in the West is ended!' Churchill broadcast to the people of

ON NOT BORING THE PANTS OFF THEM

Britain. All he said was little more than a hundred words:

> The news from France is very bad and I grieve for the
> gallant French people who have fallen into this terrible
> misfortune. Nothing will alter our feelings towards them
> or our faith that the genius of France will rise again.
> What has happened in France makes no difference to
> our actions and purpose. We have become the sole
> champions now in arms to defend the world cause. We
> shall do our best to be worthy of this high honour. We
> shall defend our island home and with the British Empire
> we shall fight on unconquerable until the curse of Hitler
> is lifted from the brows of mankind. We are sure that in
> the end all will come right.

When you want to make a letter or a report shorter, cutting
out a word here and there makes hardly any difference and
might change the feeling or meaning. Instead take out whole
sentences and complete paragraphs. Rudyard Kipling believed
that the main purpose of revision is deletion and that is a
good rule to follow. When there are less of them, every one of
our words does more work for us.

Anybody can make a mistake but justifying ourselves is
boring. Two examples from American television history show
that people can respond to someone who bungles something
and admits it right away. The stories are true although precise
details are difficult to establish.

In the days before videotape, a commercial for a cigarette
lighter was going out 'live'. The actor flipped the lighter three
times and it wouldn't work. A technician struck a match,
leant into shot and said 'Would you like a *real* light?'

A famous programme host was demonstrating a refrigerator
in a 'live' show. The new quick-release ice-tray jammed and
it took a lot of effort to yank it out. He held it up to the
camera, saying 'When they can make one that works, I'll tell
you about it'. It was a network show with high ratings and
in the control room the man from the ad agency died a
thousand deaths.

In those cases, sales of the cigarette lighter and of that make
of refrigerator went up rather than the other way. Perhaps
people responded sympathetically to the direct acceptance

76

that something had gone wrong. It is worth remembering this next time you make a mess of something. Long explanations and justifications rarely interest anyone and even judges, who are paid to listen to them, sometimes doze off.

We are all bored by a lot of facts and figures. Margaret Thatcher has admitted that one of her speeches did not go well because 'it was too full of facts and figures. The next speech I made in the House was very successful—it had only a few facts and figures.'

A successful business consultant sends his clients a short letter, after he has looked into the problem. He says, 'This is what I advise you to do'. And he tells them. The supporting facts and figures are set out separately in a detailed report, so it is clear that all the homework has been done. He knows that his clients employ him more for his recommendations than for a lengthy analysis of the problem.

A young woman used this technique to save a long tedious discussion with her husband. After dinner one evening she said:

> I believe we ought to have a dishwasher. I don't want to bore you with all the reasons why. So I've written them out on this piece of paper in case you want to go through them. But if you don't want to, that's fine. Shall we order one tomorrow?

A letter or a report can *look* boring before we start to read it. And if we think we are going to be bored, our limit of interest drops right at the outset. Before you send it out, hold up an important letter or report, not to see what it reads like, but to see what it *looks* like, before anyone reads a word.

A lot of work goes into bookjackets and the packaging of a box of chocolates or a packet of cigarettes. It does not change the contents but it does affect us and our immediate response. A letter can look efficient, reliable or friendly, just as a report can look easy to read.

When people are reading they often hear the words in their head. A letter can have a boring voice or it can sound full of energy and feeling. Short sentences, as well as being easier to understand, seem alert and vital. Compare this in a letter from a solicitor:

It is considered advisable to bring to your attention that
it cannot be assumed that the action will be successful,
although you can be assured that nothing will be
overlooked that could add to the strength of your case,
and that our best efforts will be made on your behalf.

to this rewrite:

You cannot be sure to win the action. But you can be
sure that we'll use everything that is on your side. We
promise to do our best for you.

Short words usually work better than long ones. English is
rich in monosyllables, much richer than most other languages,
and when we use them our sentences zip along. Too many
long words drag.

Some writers can make us interested in almost anything.
Alistair Cooke describes how he sits down at his typewriter,
says, 'Good evening', and goes on talking to the typewriter.
We're usually happy to listen, because his easy free-association
of one idea to the next takes us along with him all the way
from his 'Good evening' to his 'Good night'. If you can do
that, you might as well skip this chapter as you're not likely
to bore the pants off anyone. A handwritten letter from the
President of the United States or from the Princess of Wales
also has a lot going for it.

The rest of us can adapt this advice from an expert on TV
commercials: 'If you want to make thirty seconds seem a long
time, don't do much in it.' Think of it this way: if you want
to make your letters, reports and phone calls seem important,
don't write or say too much.

Readership studies show that the less separate elements
there are in an advertisement and the more they are brought
together into one simple message, the more the advertisement
will be read, remembered and acted on. Irving Berlin, who
knew that, made a fortune, lost it in the Wall Street crash
and went on to make a second fortune. 'All I need', he said,
'is a catchy phrase that anyone can understand.' His songs
never bored the pants off anyone:

There's no business like Show Business!
Oh how I hate to get up in the morning!
I'm dreaming of a White Christmas.
What'll I do when you are far away?
Isn't it a lovely day to be caught in the rain?

Irving Berling understood, without trying, the art of being simple and direct. He has sometimes been compared to another great American song writer, Cole Porter, who was sophisticated and educated at two great universities, Harvard and Yale, in contrast to the self-made Berlin. The difference, as someone commented, is that while Cole Porter 'knew how to talk to waiters, Berlin had been one'. And before anyone undervalues simplicity and directness in communication, take into account that, some years ago now, the record sales of Berlin's *White Christmas* left behind the hundred million mark.

When people are talking they use a much smaller vocabulary than when they are writing. A journalist or novelist uses many more words in their work than in their conversation. If something you write sounds heavy-going, you can lighten it by looking at all those words you would not normally use in conversation. If some of them are not essential, change them to words you would say. Then read your letter again and see the difference.

There is a well-known bookshop in the Latin Quarter of Paris, where you join one queue to give the book you have chosen to an assistant and get a bill. You leave the book behind and join another queue at the cash desk to pay. Then you come back and queue a third time, show the receipt to the assistant and take away your book. Buying a book in that shop is hard work.

A communication can be tedious like that. It can make you go backwards and forwards, trying to work it out. The most reliable rule for not boring anyone when you write or speak is to make it easy for them. They might have a lot of other things on their mind.

This chapter ends with a salute to the late Roy Brooks, a London estate agent of the 1960s, who made boring lists of properties so *un*boring that thousands of people used to read them every week in the Sunday papers. Through them he became, for a time, the best known estate agent in the country,

79

and the head of the London office of J. Walter Thompson, one of the leading American ad agencies (since subject to a daring take-over bid by a British company), chose a Roy Brooks' classified ad as one of his favourite advertisements. Here are three examples. The prices alone make nostalgic reading:

EARLS CT. Spacious 2nd/3rd flr Mais which fiercely bearded painter acquired 'from a rather dull fella in the Secret Service. I sculp a bit in wood so I've been able to do some smashing fitted cupbds in kit.' Artistic arch links 2 rec rms to form fab STUDIO rec rm. 3 Bedrms. Bathrm. kit. steel sink unit. SUNBATHING ROOF. Lse 64 yrs. GR £19 ONLY £6,995 even try an offer.

'I was a teenage literary agent' confessed Mrs L, gazing thro' the wall of glass in her new Nursery/Study, at the garden. 'A pity we had to cut the walnut tree down.' The rest is XVIIIth CENT. A small house of alleged royal ownership in the days of Kew Palace. On Kew Green & at rear looking to River and over Tennis Courts. An enchanting dble drawing rm, clkrm, and mod kit. 2 principal bedrms, small 3rd bedrm for child or dwarf lodger. All the class of living behind a Georgian fanlight for less than the price of a suburban villa. Only £8,995 FREEHOLD. View Sun.

There is a fashionable odour of decay in this PIMLICO PERIOD RES. 8/9 rms in horrible state of decoration. Innocent of all modern amenities. Nature has fought back in the gdn—& won. Single family occupation only as subletting not allowed in this fashionable slum development. BARGAIN £8,450. Lse 80 yrs. G.R. £50. Key Brooks.

In case you are wondering whether they sold a lot of houses and flats, here is the answer: they did.

The way to give words added value

There is a world of difference between saying that apples contain vitamins and natural sugar and that inspired piece of early marketing know-how 'An apple a day keeps the doctor away'.

In economics *added value* is doing something to raw material that makes it worth more. Virgin wool is dyed and woven into cloth, which adds value to it, more value still if people like the pattern and the colour. Value is added to wine in casks by bottling it, more value still if there's a good label on the bottle.

It is an exciting concept to think of words as the raw materials of communication. They acquire added value when they are put together in a way that makes people read them, listen to them, be inspired by them, moved by them or influenced by them.

It was once said that Webster's Dictionary contains all the words in the English language. That's not true, of course, not even for the twenty heavy volumes of *The Oxford English Dictionary*. Words are all over the place and no one can ever find them all. But a small pocket dictionary gives you enough words to make language do a great deal for you. The moment you put some of those words into a simple phrase that has meaning for someone else, you have given them added value.

Good ideas add a lot of value to words: they take something ordinary and make it dramatic, new and alive. You can tell a girl that here is a hair-rinse that leaves your hair fair. An American advertising writer injected drama and a sense of adventure:

> You've got only one life to live—so why not live it as a *blonde*?

Anyone can say the engine of a Rolls-Royce is so quiet you can hardly hear it. David Ogilvy, a Scotsman who opened his own advertising agency in New York of all places, said it this way:

> At 60 miles an hour the loudest noise in this new Rolls-Royce comes from the electric clock.

This became a classic advertisement, quoted in ad agencies all over the world. It was made even more famous by the legendary story that David Ogilvy told about it. When with some pride he submitted the ad for approval, the senior Rolls-

Royce executive resident in New York, 'that austere British engineer', as Ogilvy called him, hesitated for a moment or two, frowned and said thoughtfully 'We really must do something to improve our clock.'

The Walls Meat Company could have said their meat pies have a lot of meat in them. Someone had a better idea:

Walls Meat Pies—Light on Pastry

Heavy on Meat

Avis are not the biggest in the car-hire business. A clever idea turned a negative into a plus, adding a lot of value to plain words—'We're No.2. So we try harder.' *We try harder* became a catchphrase and doubled the Avis share of the car-hire market.

Remember this book some years ago: *Everything You Always Wanted to Know About Sex but Were Afraid to Ask?* The last five words add so much. They link up with those unexpressed doubts and uncertainties that many people feel about sex.

Poets add more value to words than anyone else, because their words can give us a new insight. No one knows how poetry works. It has something to do with the rhythm of the words, the choice of words or the use of an unexpected word that jolts us into awareness. When W. H. Auden writes about being in bed and making love, the rhythm is quiet and reflective:

Learn what love alone can teach:
Happy on a tousled bed.

The unexpected word *tousled* gives us a little shock of recognition and connects with our own experience.

John Tessimond, another poet, was an advertising copywriter, so when he writes about love, his words are simple. The added value comes from the rhythm and transparent sincerity:

No more time or place
Once I see her face.
Sorrow, doubt and fear
Leave when she is near.
Warm, her eyes and hand,
Wordless, understand.

Robert W. Bork, a Solicitor General of the United States, said
'If people buy little daydreams with advertising, I don't know
that we ought to be terribly upset about it.' John Tessimond,
the poet, wrote lyrical advertising that added value to words
by adding romance. Here's one of his ads for shoes:

THE GIRL WHO WANTED THE MOON IN HER HAND

Once upon a time there was a girl
who had been invited to go dancing
one night in December.

Then, if never again, she wanted
the moon in her hand and the world
at her feet . . . the world and one
man especially.

She found the dress in Paris,
the stockings, the perfume.

And the *shoes*?
The shoes were in her mind's eye.
Light and slight as air.
Slim and young and soft.
White and gold and gleaming.

We found her the shoes,
Golden-strapped, featherlight but firm.
Held firm by the fine spun strength
of white nylon mesh.

Shoes to dance in till dawn.

A lot of unknown, unsung people have given words added
value by inventing catchphrases. They present us 'free, gratis
and for nothing' with an off-the-peg stock of good ways to
give words the added value of sharpness and wit:

Hold your horses!
Let it all hang out.

85

Money for old rope.
It fell off the back of a lorry.
I wasn't born yesterday.
Run it up on the flagpole and see who salutes it.
Don't rock the boat!

And there are a whole lot more where they came from.

How can you give your words added value? Not many of us have the intuition of a poet and maybe you cannot snatch out of the clouds a brilliant idea just when you want one. But there is a simple approach that can step up the value of words any time you want to use it.

Words always take on added value when they appeal to someone's motives and interests. When your words do that, they leap up in value. The first step is to think what the other person wants. Some psychologists assert that if we peel back enough layers, we find our motive for doing anything is self-interest. It is complex enough to try to penetrate the meaning of life without having such a large spanner thrown into the works. There is no need to deny the existence of altruism, objective truth, beauty and faith.

The day-to-day struggle in the jungle we live in is something else. Dr Edward de Bono, an expert on the processes of creative thinking, says without hesitation 'In some form or another the pay-off is the reason for all action.' We may not want to go all the way with that, but that's how it is so much of the time in the world of letters, memos, meetings and telephone calls. If these are to be successful, we must be aware of the motives of the people we are dealing with. Then even the simplest words take on added value.

When Guinness first started advertising in 1928, a couple of copywriters went from pub to pub, talking to Guinness drinkers. They kept finding people who thought Guinness did them good. That's what people wanted so that's what the copywriters said—as simply as possible:

GUINNESS IS GOOD FOR YOU

That simple statement remained the Guinness slogan for decades.

In the far-off days when petrol was cheap and drivers were more interested in speed and performance than miles per gallon, Shell offered it to them in four easy words:

86

THAT'S SHELL—THAT WAS!

If something costs a lot of money, people want it to last a long time. Years ago, four words made that promise memorably:

A DIAMOND IS FOREVER

You will still see those words at the bottom of De Beers' advertisements for diamonds. Evidence and research always show that when it comes to adding value to words, simplicity leaves clever intellectual ideas miles behind.

We can get more ideas from the ways advertising uses psychology and research to locate and define motives. Because an advertising campaign that makes the wrong appeal can waste millions, advertisers employ psychologists to probe deeper, below the rational obvious levels, down into the unconscious.

The American writer Vance Packard, whose book *The Hidden Persuaders* attacked the use of psychoanalysis by advertising agencies, reluctantly accepted:

> . . . that some pushing and hauling of the citizenry is probably necessary to make our $400,000,000,000-a-year economy work.

(That figure was quoted in 1957, by the way.) But he rejected the use of psychoanalysis to sell goods by using people's unconscious fears and anxieties. Without going as far as that, some knowledge of how we function can make our communications with other human beings more valuable for us and to them. It is intelligent and reasonable to develop some awareness of motives and needs, so that we can give our words added value by making the right appeals instead of the wrong ones.

In the advertising business they call it motivational research. One technique is the depth-interview, a one-to-one meeting between a psychologist and someone who has volunteered to talk about why they buy certain products. Not far from New York, six hundred feet up overlooking the Hudson River, was the Institute for Motivational Research. It was never an academic institute but a successful business that helped advertisers to understand their customers' motives. Other research companies sell different methods. There is a lot of disagreement even among the experts.

When the American Jesuits wanted to get more members, they turned to Dr Ernest Dichter, founder of the Institute for Motivational Research Inc. He suggested 'Don't offer them a life after death, but a full and satisfying life on this earth—the same as industry.'

Dr Dichter, who early in his career was a psychoanalyst in that well-spring of psychoanalysis, Vienna, stressed the importance of emotional security in every sales approach. Another psychologist advises 'If you want people to do something, you have got to help them feel right about doing it.'

Airlines have for a long time been interested in attitudes towards flying. Some years ago psychological research carried out by the University of London suggested that passengers in some way associate a flight with the idea of an operation in hospital. The pilot has the image of the surgeon, the man in charge. Stewardesses fit into the role of nurses. You can see how these unconscious connections could be made. When you enter an aircraft, you are to some extent helpless. From then on, other people are in charge and your life is at stake. Airlines latched on to this by stressing safety and care. In those days, when BOAC existed as the British airline for long-distance transcontinental flights, they used the reassuring slogan: BOAC TAKES GOOD CARE OF YOU.

Manufacturers of cakemixes also found they were getting into deep emotional stuff. A social psychologist advised them that a woman baking a cake makes some kind of a connection with the birth of a child. It is still said in the north of England that a pregnant girl 'has a bun in the oven'. Cakemix manufacturers accepted that it was good for business to help women feel more creative by letting them add their own eggs or milk to the mixture.

Some of the conclusions of motivational research are bizarre. One expert admitted 'Sometimes, I think we can go in too deep.' We do not have to believe all of it. But some of the ideas are interesting and encourage us to go a little below the surface ourselves in our own attempts to understand how our words can get through.

The next time you write for a job, or ask a girl out to dinner, or a man home for a drink, there is no need to dive into the deep dark waters of depth-psychology. Down there even the experts get lost and confused. But more of us have the capacity, through understanding ourselves, to become more aware of the human psyche, that blend of emotional, intellectual and instinctive forces within us that make us respond, react, accept, reject, love and hate.

It may be comforting to think that we behave rationally, that we always know what we are doing and why we are doing it. But what is rational to you might not be rational to someone else. Our words start to take on added value from the moment we understand and accept that the other person will not automatically see things in the way we want them to.

The ancient Greeks can teach us something about this too. Protagoras held that truth is not cut and dried and so often it depends on how we see it. Everything has to relate to man: *Man is the measure of all things*. At times, we must seek to understand and value other perspectives, other points of view. The Scottish psychiatrist, Dr R. D. Laing, believes that what society calls madness can sometimes be a perfectly clear and consistent view of life; it is just a completely different view from the one that most of us live with.

How can we make use of this when we put words together for something as practical as getting a complaint dealt with, putting up a recommendation to the board of directors or asking our wife or husband to accept that we don't want to go out this evening? We want our words to cross the gap between the way we see things and the way the other person sees them.

Suppose our heart is set on carrying through a new project and we want the go-ahead. The board wants profit-margins increased, which requires more sales or lower costs. If we use our words to offer them what they want, we start to close the gap between us. Making words appeal to someone else is giving them added value.

It is not always enough to tell people the facts. We have to say how those facts offer them something they want. There is a world of difference between saying that apples contain vitamins and natural sugar and that inspired early marketing know-how 'An apple a day keeps the doctor away'.

Back in the early days of vacuum-cleaners, there was an unknown unsung hero of marketing, a long since forgotten door-to-door salesman who thought of taking with him on his calls a bag of dirt. To the dismay of the housewife, he spread it on the carpet and then let her see how easily the vacuum-cleaner sucked it up. More than half a century later, advertising experts are paid high fees to advise that the most effective way to sell on television is to demonstrate. The old vacuum-cleaner salesman knew that from the seat of his pants.

Demonstration takes the facts and shows what they will do for us. An old American commercial for Volkswagen used a minute on television to demonstrate something without saying anything, except asking one short question. The camera pans slowly over an icy scene until it reaches a VW buried in a snowdrift. The announcer asks: 'How does the guy who drives the snowplough *get* to the snowplough?' A man gets into the Volkswagen, starts it first time and drives off.

Another American commercial, for DieHard batteries, sold a lot of batteries by demonstrating that they live up to their name. Five cars, all with flat batteries, are started one after the other with the same two-year-old DieHard.

You can use this principle with words, as a girl did when she wanted to get a job in films. She wrote to a film producer offering to work a week for nothing to demonstrate that she was efficient, quick-thinking and reliable. He took her up on it. At the end of the week, he decided to pay her and give her the job.

Words can demonstrate things. A secretary wrote for a job and instead of saying her shorthand speed was 120 words a minute, she showed what it would do for someone:

You can dictate to me at two words a second, and when you see it typed out it will usually be accurate, word for word as you dictated it.

Everybody is selling something. Go to any meeting and you hear people selling ideas, theories, points of view or attitudes. Every high street is full of shop windows inviting us to buy. Every politician sells the advantages of electing him and his party. The Queen in her Christmas Day broadcast sells goodwill and national unity. Successful selling with words, as with demonstrations, starts with recognition of what the other person wants. Otherwise why should anyone listen to us?

A few years ago an international financier advertised for staff to sell his investment schemes, using the headline:

DO YOU SINCERELY WANT TO BE RICH?

For most of us that is too blatant to be comfortable, although it is probably true that money is the pay-off that attracts people more than any other. But it is a substitute for the things most of us really want, which are security, happiness and peace of mind. If you can offer those things, with sincerity and honesty, they will always add value to your words.

It is normal to want to be liked. Generally people prefer to say *yes* rather than *no* and are often more willing to do something for us than we realise. Many times it makes little difference to them: it could mean nothing more than walking along to the next office and speaking to someone, or picking up the phone and speaking to another department. People will often help if we ask in the right way.

Put yourself at the receiving end of the following two requests.

We are in a hurry for this so could you send it as soon as you can?

We are in a fix over this and every day counts. Will you please do what you can to help us?

They both came in the same post addressed to a busy production manager. The second request got priority.

Making the right appeal is everything and it can save lives, as well as selling goods. This was a slogan for a road safety campaign:

TEACH YOUR CHILDREN
THE GREEN KNIGHT SAFETY RULES

Something like this would have offered more to parents:

HELP YOUR CHILDREN GET HOME SAFE

When you write a letter, or make a phone call, asking for something to be done for you or to help someone else, look for the basic factor most relevant to the person you are writing or speaking to. There are usually a number of factors and it is worth working at choosing the most effective ones.

The peace of the world can depend upon this, although then it is more likely to be called diplomacy. It is nonetheless exactly the same approach. Dr Henry Kissinger, who was

Secretary of State for Richard Nixon, appeared to be able to work near miracles of persuasion. He was called the 'special negotiator' and was awarded the Nobel Peace Prize in 1973 in recognition of his exceptional ability for presenting the factors of a dispute so that each side saw the benefits to themselves of coming to an agreement.

This way of adding value to words has never been put with more commercial force than in the concept of the USP, a theory of advertising propounded by Rosser Reeves, the adman who produced the television commercials for Eisenhower's presidential campaign. If you haven't come across it, USP stands for *Unique Selling Proposition*. It is old-fashioned jargon these days but whatever else they call it, ad agencies still scratch around desperately looking for the same thing: something specific that a product or service can offer that nothing else can. Here are some examples:

INTRODUCING THE ONLY SANDWICH BAG
THAT REALLY KEEPS ITS MOUTH SHUT
Ziploc Sandwich Bags with a zipper-like seal that shuts the bag.

IF YOU'RE ROBBED ON HOLIDAY, THIS
TRAVELLER'S CHEQUE MAKES SURE YOUR
HOLIDAY GOES ON
American Express traveller's cheques offer a full refund usually on the same day you lose them.

THE LAST GAS STATION FOR 500 MILES
Sign outside a garage in the Australian outback.

Daddy's away abroad, so I'm the only one
who can give you a cuppa in bed on Sunday.
A ten-year-old boy to his mother, making out a case for extra pocket money.

I'm the greatest!
Muhammad Ali.

The weakest kind of advertising is called *me too* advertising. It says 'You can buy this in a lot of other places but I also sell it'. Many sales letters say, in effect, 'We want you to buy what we are selling'. The inevitable reaction is, 'Thank you very much. But why should I?'

Every time we want something done there has to be a reason why, or our letter, conversation or report ends up as another *me too* communication. It joins the queue with all the others unless we find something to make our case a special one.

There are times, of course, when there is nothing special that we can offer, except the way we offer it. David Ogilvy, the British advertising man who made good in New York, was ' . . . astonished to find how many manufactures, on both sides of the Atlantic, still believe that women can be persuaded by logic and argument to buy one brand in preference to another, even if the two brands are technically identical'.

When it is not what you say but the way you say it, you are involved in building an *image*. A famous example is what David Ogilvy did for a little known shirt manufacturer. In every advertisement, he used a man with a black eyepatch, who became *The Man in the Hathaway Shirt*, an image of confidence, virility and courage. It caught on, helped by Moshe Dayan, the herioc Israeli general at the time, who always wore a black eyepatch.

Ogilvy even ran full-page colour advertisements in *The New Yorker* without a single word, not even the name *Hathaway*. But everyone knew it was a Hathaway shirt in the ad, because the man had a black eyepatch.

People have loyalty towards a brand of cigarettes, although tests show that often they cannot tell their favourite brand from several others. Mary Wells Lawrence, as a leading woman in American advertising, explained 'you have to realise that when you buy a cigarette, part of what you buy is the image of yourself smoking that cigarette'.

Benson and Hedges cigarettes come in a gold-coloured box and gold is the theme of all the advertising. On posters and in colour ads, they can leave out the brand name so long as there is enough gold around. In 1978 when the gold treasures of El Dorado were brought to London for a dazzling show at the Royal Academy, you can guess whose name was publicly linked with the exhibition.

We cannot help being in the image business. Our image is projected by the clothes we wear, the food we eat, the places we are seen in—and the words we use. Try this test next time you get a letter from someone you don't know. Forget the facts it is telling you and ask what it tells you about the person who wrote it. Now take one of your own letters and try to read it as if you do not know who wrote it. Don't look at the arguments and requests you are making. Just ask what kind of a person would have written that letter, and is that image going to help your case?

Compare these extracts from two letters received by a finance company:

Letter 1

I understand that you are sometimes prepared to advance capital to people who want to expand their business.

My wife and I run two sandwich bars in this town, serving sandwiches and coffee for lunch to men and women who work in nearby offices. Our turnover has been going up each year for the last three years, and we have also started a send-out service of coffee in plastic mugs with lids.

We hope to open two more bars of the same kind in other parts of the town and we have been looking out for suitable premises.

Letter 2

My wife and I have spent two years working in Health Food Restaurants, because we want to make a go of one for ourselves.

We are young, in our early thirties, full of enthusiasm ourselves for eating fresh salads, wholemeal bread, free-range eggs, cheeses on the rind and other kinds of natural foods. That is the kind of food we are going to serve to our customers, who will be people working in offices.

We know from our experience and from asking around that more and more people are interested in eating natural foods, so the tide is going our way.

We are confident that we have found the perfect premises. There are a lot of office people working in the area, but there is no other Health Food Restaurant or salad bar anywhere near.

They are both good letters but what would you think the writers are like? The finance company executive thought the first letter came from a rather quiet middle-aged couple, who were running a couple of ordinary sandwich bars. The couple who sent the second letter seemed to be young, go-ahead and full of good ideas and ambition.

He was wrong about the first couple. They are still in their twenties. Their two sandwich bars are attractive, with old stripped-pine counters and stools. They sell a variety of delicious sandwiches with inventive fillings, such as shrimps with home-made mayonnaise and shredded lettuce or ham and pineapple or cheese with grated nuts and dates. The second couple turned out to be much as he had expected, lively, with a lot of drive and energy.

It is not the information in those two letters that makes the difference. In fact, the writer of *Letter 1* had more to offer, because the business was already started and going well. The letters gave different impressions because of the *images* they projected of the people who had written them.

A run-of-the-mill expected way of putting down what you want to say usually produces a rather low-level response. One of the cleverest creative men in American advertising was asked to address an advertising convention. He called his talk *How to be Different*. Sometimes it takes a lot of effort and head-breaking to find a different and effective way of saying something but it is worth it because of all the added value your words take along with them.

Many makes of cars talk about good road-holding. The writer of the ads for the Chevrolet *Camaro* worked hard at being different:

GO OUT AND HUG A ROAD YOU LIKE
Roads and Camaros.
When it comes to hugging, there hasn't been
anything like them since Romeo and Juliet.

He gives all the reasons: steel-belted radial tyres, a front stabiliser bar, low lines, power steering and a positive drive. At the end, he says pick the model you want and 'Then go out hug a road!'

For years building societies all seemed much the same, monumentally dull organisations. The old and respectable Woolwich Equitable Building Society was one of the first to decide to be different. They let their hair down in a series of fifteen-second spots on television, using stock comedy situations to put over the alliterative slogan 'We're with the Woolwich!' One commercial showed a pantomime in rehearsal:

| *Producer* | Are you Widder Twankey? |
| *Panto dame* | No, I'm Widder Woolwich! |

Another showed a group of Martians parking their flying saucer:

| *Traffic warden* | Oi! Are you lot with that flying saucer? |
| *Martians* | No, we're with the Woolwich! |

It was hardly brilliant stuff, nor was it very funny, but at the time building societies didn't do that kind of thing. The Woolwich was breaking fresh ground and Donald Markham their chief executive hoped that:

> Familiarity and good humour might suggest that such things as security and financial returns could go with the everyday, with shopping expeditions, with people of all types and ages.

For the Woolwich being different paid off as research showed that more people were entrusting their money to them.

Since then, of course, building societies, banks, and the most sedate financial institutions have been tumbling over themselves, desperately trying to look lively, trendy and laid back. The resulting advertising has occasionally been over the top or pointless, but that is the way with pendulums, once they start swinging.

When we use our imagination and intelligence to give our words added value, they bring us what we want and may help others. This is not to counsel unscrupulous selling and persuasion. Words have a potentiality for evil as well as for good, but they cannot be neutral; they affect people one way or another. We have to start by having something to say. The next thing is to look for the value of what we say, not to ourselves but to the other person. 'Do not', Bernard Shaw grumbled, 'do unto others as you would they should do unto you. Their tastes may be different.'

How to come to a good end

The most famous exit line in the history of films was Mae West's in She Done Him Wrong. *She filled the doorway like the stuffing in a vol-au-vent, wiggled everything from fingertips to toenails, and invited us to 'Come up 'n' see me sometime!'*

Your last sentence is the last thing people read. It is your last chance to get through to them before signing your name. The last thing you say on the telephone before you hang up is the last thought you leave in the other person's mind. Your last words as you are leaving a meeting or an interview make the final impression for you. The way we end something can be even more important than the way we begin it, because people remember how things end.

Research on television commercials shows that the beginning and the end of a commercial are usually remembered best. The beginning because it is something new; and the end because that is what viewers see just before the next commercial comes up to take their attention. It is the same with the end of your letter: that is the last thing someone takes in before going on to something else.

You cannot count on anyone reading anything a second time. At the best, people might skim through your letter again to remind themselves of what it is about. When that happens, they are more likely to read again in full your last sentence or last paragraph. It is common to hope that the end of a letter or a report will tell us all we need to know about it.

If you watch people choosing a book in a library or bookshop, you will often see them glancing through it, looking through the list of chapter headings, and then turning to the last page. They want to see what comes at the end.

Perhaps this is to avoid disappointment, because it's one thing to make a good beginning and something else to carry the same quality all the way through to the end.

When we say 'All's well that ends well', we mean that even if things go wrong somewhere along the line, if it works out all right in the end, then we don't mind so much what has gone before. Our own experience confirms this. What at the time seems a disaster can be forgotten if something good comes out of it in the end. A relationship can go through storms and tempests but if somehow it survives with some understanding and harmony, the past sufferings seem unimportant. In show business, when everything is going wrong at the dress rehearsal, the cast and the desperate director are sustained by the determination and hope that it will be 'all right on the night'. That's all that matters.

In communication, getting off to a bad start is a setback,

but coming to a bad end can mean total failure. When you are writing something or speaking to someone, you cannot always be sure to say just the right things, no matter how hard you try. But if the last thing you say pulls it all together for you, your communication stands a good chance of success.

Many letters, meetings, telephone calls and love-affairs come to a bad end or just fizzle out. What happens is that we use all our energy writing or dictating an important letter, making a difficult telephone call or coping with an interview that a lot depends on. When it is nearly over, there is such a sense of relief that it's easy to be careless about what we say from then on. Or we fall back on some how's-your-father? banality that means nothing and is a weak conclusion to our letter or conversation.

Most of us have experienced a letdown feeling after a telephone call, because we have allowed it to end in a feeble inconsequential way. We want to phone back to put it right but it is too late. The moment has gone. Even after a good meeting or interview, we can shut the conference room or office door behind us, with the uneasy thought that we have muffed the last minute or two. We have relaxed our concentration too soon instead of holding it to the last moment. In golf and tennis, and most other ball games, it is important, even *after* striking the ball, to follow through, to carry the stroke all the way to the end.

It is human nature to sustain an almost superhuman effort as long as it seems necessary and then let go completely. Sprinters often flake out immediately they breast the tape, and oarsmen slump over their oars at the end of a boatrace. This happens in communication. It is quite a strain to write a letter that means a great deal to us, or to go through a meeting, an interview or even a telephone call that could affect our lives. So when it seems to be over, it is natural to feel relieved, although we still haven't written the last sentence, left the office or hung up the phone.

In communication, as in most other activities, following through all the way to the end is part of the action. When it is an important letter, treat the last sentence with a lot of respect. It is far too valuable to waste on anything like these examples:

I hope you will give this every consideration.
(From a man asking for a transfer from the north of England to the London office.)

Looking forward to hearing from you at your convenience.
(From the director of a company offering a demonstration of a new type of photocopying machine.)

I am looking forward to receiving your application.
(From the head of one of the biggest chargecard services in the world.)

Do send me your subscription form today.
(From the circulation director of a leading US business magazine.)

Once again, please forgive me for not turning up for the appointment.
(From a girl who didn't arrive for an interview for a job.)

Although those were important letters to the people who wrote them, the endings are banal. They might just as well have been left out altogether because they add nothing of value. This is a waste because the last sentence of a letter can be decisive. At the least, it can make a final contact with the reader and in some cases it can make the difference between the whole thing being put on one side or something being done about it then and there.

Last words are important. Actresses and actors love a good exit line because they leave the stage not with a whimper but with a bang that makes an impact for them on the audience. One of the great exit lines in literature is in Charles Dickens' *A Tale of Two Cities*. Sydney Carton, the wastrel of an English barrister, says this, as he saves another man's life by taking his place on the scaffold:

> It is a far, far better thing that I do than I have ever done; it is a far, far better rest that I go to, than I have ever known.

We are left feeling that he has, in the end, made up for everything that has gone before.

The most famous exit line in the history of films was Mae West's in *She Done Him Wrong*. She filled a doorway like the stuffing in a vol-au-vent, wiggled everything from fingertips to toenails and invited us to:

> Come up 'n' see me sometime!

There is an easy way to give any important communication a good exit line. You do it by asking *What do I want to happen next?* What do you want to happen after whoever it is finishes reading your letter, after you hang up the phone or leave an office after a meeting? Sometimes it is worth writing down beforehand the answer to that question so that you are clear about it. Then all you have to do is embody that answer in your last sentence.

Advertisers know all about this. Delegates at international advertising film festivals in Cannes or Venice come away after a week of looking at commercials from all over the world, knowing how to say in a whole lot of languages *Buy some tomorrow!*

That pay-off comes up at the end of TV commercials from every country. It is what the advertising business is about. However calm and distinguished some advertisers pretend to be, that's what they want to happen, that's what they pay for. A New Year commercial, announcing a special offer for one week, ended:

Run! (Do not walk!) to your nearest drugstore and ask for . . . !

That may sound over the top but it conveyed to housewives the sense of urgency the advertiser wanted.

The most effective endings are action endings. You have someone's attention for a few minutes. Whoever it is has stopped whatever they were doing to read your letter or listen to you. Very soon the person who can help you will be interested in something else and for the time being will forget about you. If it is at all possible or appropriate, use your last sentence to ask them to do something. Make it as specific as you can and as short as you can.

Once again Winston Churchill provides a marvellous demonstration of how to do it. He is replying to President Roosevelt. 'We shall not fail or falter' he says, 'We shall not weaken or tire . . .' Then comes his last sentence, short, definite and asking for action: 'Give us the tools, and we will finish the job.'

It is well known in advertising practice that a coupon at the end of an advertisement multiplies the returns not just by two or three but by ten times and more. It gives readers something definite to do, instead of leaving them to think about something they might do later on. We have all seen advertisements and thought 'I must do something about that'. The moment passes and we forget. So advertisers include a 'freephone' number or a 'freepost' address to make it as easy as possible for a reader to do something right away.

A former Canadian mounted policeman got a job in advertising by sending up a note by hand to the head of Lord and Thomas, at the time the most successful advertising agency in the United States. His last sentence read:

> If you wish to know what advertising is, send the word YES down by the messenger.

The request for immediate action worked. The boss came down himself and over a drink in a nearby bar heard the oracle. In case you are interested, he was told that advertising is 'Salesmanship in print', which still holds up as a good definition.

Here are some other examples of endings that led to immediate and specific action. A mother wrote to the headmaster of her daughter's school. Sally, her daughter, who was fourteen, showed exceptional musical talent and her mother wanted her to have extra piano lessons in place of other subjects. She ended her letter:

> I know it is not easy to rearrange time-tables for individual pupils, so I would not ask it unless I felt it is really important to Sally. If you can do this for her, we should all be very grateful. If you want to discuss it, please telephone me. I shall stay in all this morning, waiting.

The managing director of a medium-sized manufacturing company received a complaint from an important customer. His reply ended:

> You are a special customer, so I want to put the matter right and see that it never happens again. Would you let

me send over a working party of three to meet their opposite numbers working for you, so that we can see how to stop anything going wrong in future?

Here is a list of dates and times when our people are able, ready and very willing to come along. Please tick the most convenient time and FAX it back to me personally.

A girl sent a good promotion idea to the managing director of a store. Her letter ended:

Somebody is going to cash-in on this idea. Before anyone else does, can I tell you more about it? I'll telephone your secretary Wednesday morning, 7 May. If it's all right with you, please give her a time when I can come to see you.

This is the ending of a letter from a wine merchant selling off, after Christmas, what are known in the trade as *bin-ends*:

These left-overs are marked well down in price. We have a lot of customers, so the best we can do is to make it 'first come first served'.

This is a real chance to buy better wines at the same price as you've been paying for something much more ordinary. We'd love to think of you drinking them. But help us not to disappoint you, by going through the list now. And please send your order *today*—and be one of the lucky ones.

Those are four different situations. But the endings all do one thing: they ask for action and make it clear what that action is. Three of the endings do even better. They give a time-limit. Always look for the possibility of giving a time-limit, when you can do that without arousing resentment in the other person, because a time-limit is the most effective way of getting action. A distinguished newspaper editor used to say to young reporters who were late with their copy 'I don't want it good. I don't want it bad. I want it in half an hour!'

There is an infallible test of the effectiveness of any last sentence. Cover it up. If it makes no real difference to the letter, you have come to a bad end. Try this on the four letters quoted above. Cover the last sentence and you will see there is a loss of energy, drive and purpose. If that happens when you cover one of your last sentences, you have a good ending and can send off your letter with a good heart.

When you are making an important telephone call, you have the advantage of being able to plan it. You can write down what you are going to say to begin with; and you can write down what you are going to say at the end. Then it is there in front of you, even if you have to change it round a little to meet the circumstances.

You can plan your last words at an interview, so that you go out saying something that will help your case. When you have said it, the best thing is to finish and say no more. A feeling of insecurity often makes us go on beyond the point of real usefulness. That can easily make an encounter end on a weak note instead of a positive one.

At that macabre banquet in Macbeth's palace, when Banquo's ghost turns up as an uninvited and unwelcome guest, the other visitors are slow to leave. Lady Macbeth tells them not to hang about:

> Stand not upon the order of your going
> But go at once.

At a meeting or an interview, if you have come up with a good exit line, the next thing to do is to exit.

Here is a collection of good ways that people have ended meetings and interviews. We start with a president at the end of an annual general meeting:

> Before I sit down, can I tell you this? We think of the shareholders as our friends, because without you there would be no business. At some time, during every board meeting, I ask this question: 'Will it be good for the shareholders?'

A headmistress ended her address to parents:

> We see ourselves as working with you to help your sons

and daughters. Will you think of yourselves as working with us? When there are disagreements and irritations, please remember this—we are both on the *same* side.

A representative from the shop-floor ended his case to the works manager for a new procedure to increase production and hence productivity bonuses:

> Give us a chance to try this out for two weeks. If there are any headaches to begin with, I'll work late to put them right and give my overtime pay to any charity you name.

A girl at the end of an interview for a job:

> I've got enthusiasm and I want to do well. That can't be bad, can it?

We learn something important from readership tests of advertisements. They show what happens when people read our letters and memos. Their interest is at a higher level to begin with because they are reading something new; and as we have seen, our first sentence can make that interest much higher still. They read the body of the letter to see what it says and then, towards the end, attention and interest tend to fall away.

Observe yourself when you are reading letters and you will often see the flow of your interest following the same downward curve towards the end. Suppose it is a letter giving an estimate for building work. You want to see right away how much it is. From then on, your interest and attention drop away and you just glance at the last sentence. Research and recall tests of advertisements regularly show this pattern.

We are more successful at getting through to someone when we are sensitive to how they are likely to respond at each stage. If we change the usual response by lifting their attention at the end of an important letter, we leave them more receptive towards us.

We have noted that a request for action right at the end of a letter gets the adrenalin flowing. Another good ending is to ask a question. It works in headlines and it also works in last sentences.

This is a question at the end of a letter from a bank manager introducing customers to a new automated cashier system:

> We look after your money 24 hours a day, so don't you think it is fair you should be able to have access to it 24 hours a day?

A secretarial agency wrote to local firms and also used a question to end their letter:

> Do you want temporary secretaries and typists who are good value because they are thoroughly tested *before* they are sent to you?

A letter from a parliamentary candidate to his constituents finished up:

> After all, do you want a member who believes he is in Parliament to look after your interests *more than anything else?*

Asking a question at the end of a letter is like keeping up your voice at the end of a sentence: it keeps people with you.

People at the top everywhere are under a lot of strain and the pressure is always on them to turn to the next thing. They are making decisions all day long and it is a relief for them not to have to think something through right away. At the end of a communication, try if you can to make a positive suggestion about what the next step could be, even if it's no more than 'Please let me know a time when I can come to talk about this'. That might take you further along in the direction you want to go.

In our lives we do not write only business letters; we write to people we love and to our friends. Sometimes these letters have to traverse the world and take with them comfort, good humour and greetings. When we are writing to someone we care about, the ending of our letter is just as important because it can carry our feelings along with it.

In New York a girl in hospital received a letter from her mother in England. This was the last sentence:

> When you are feeling low, remember this my dear—I am with you all the time.

Sydney Smith, a lovable and good-natured clergyman, gave this advice at the end of a short note to Lucy, who was on her way to Boulogne:

> Don't marry anybody who has not a tolerable understanding and a thousand a year, and God bless you, dear child!

In 1835, when that letter was written, a thousand pounds a year could set you up in luxury and comfort.

This is the last sentence of a much sadder letter. The courage and feeling of the man who wrote it still come through. In the best tradition of good communication, Robert Falcon Scott, near to the South Pole, uses his last sentence for the most important request he has left:

> These rough notes and our dead bodies must tell the tale, but surely, surely, a great rich country like ours will see that those who are dependent on us are properly provided for.

Next, the ending of a letter full of good humour and friendliness. Charles MacArthur and Ben Hecht were journalists in Chicago, who worked together and wrote comedies together. MacArthur had taken James, his sixteen-year-old son, on holiday to Venezuela. His letter back to his old friend, Ben Hecht, ends up:

> Jim won the ship's ping-pong contest. He doesn't want to be called Jamie any more, and is chasing a blonde my size. Time sure flies.
> Sunburned salutes to you all.

Ending telephone calls is difficult. We all know how easy it is to let them ramble on until the whole point and all the feeling are lost. Or we end them abruptly so the other person feels cut off. The only way to do better is to be alert and decide in advance how you want to leave the person you are speaking to. Someone I love once said this to me at the end of a long-distance call and I still remember it warmly:

That was a marvellous conversation. It was just like having you here in the room beside me.

I heard another telephone call end like this. It was a man talking to his wife, whose father had just died:

If I were with you, darling, I'd put my arms around you and hold you very close. Imagine that's just what I'm doing right now.

The telephone can be as cold and sterile as a surgeon's scalpel or it can be as warm as a red rose. It all depends upon what we say and how we say it.

We have to work hard to arrive at a good ending to any communication. We have to think of what we want that valuable last sentence or paragraph to do for us or for someone else. And we have to find the words in time. The rewards make it all worthwhile, for if we get it right our communication stands a good chance of bringing about what we want to happen next. Or it brings warmth or comfort into someone's life.

Almost anything is better than letting a letter, a meeting or a telephone call drag on. 'Begin at the beginning', the King said gravely in *Alice in Wonderland*, 'and go on till you come to the end. Then stop.'

I've got the message.

Psycholinguistics

Certain words and ideas make us react in a particular way, leave us more helpful or less helpful, move us towards something or pull us away from it. When we want to get through to people, we can use these forces to work for us.

Dictionaries deal with the meaning of words but that is only part of the picture, because words contain something else. Dr Carl Gustav Jung, the psychologist and healer, discovered that words are also full of symbols. By a symbol, he meant something that triggers off a response deep within us so that we react, often without knowing why. For Jung:

> . . . a word or an image is symbolic when it implies something more than its obvious and immediate meaning. It has a wider 'unconscious' aspect that is never precisely defined or fully explained.

Psycholinguistics is the study of this other aspect of language, the interaction between words and our minds and emotions. There are hardly any places where it is taught and you may not find *psycholinguistics* in your dictionary, although some dictionaries now include it. We have to be aware of it if we want our words to get through to other people in the right way.

All the time we are reading or listening, writing or speaking, we are involved in psycholinguistics because we are affected and are affecting others, not only by what the words are saying but by their emotional charge and the underlying meanings people associate with them.

Many words are like stones with three facets. The first facet is the straightforward meaning you find in the dictionary. The second is something symbolic that affects us in a rather vague way that we do not fully understand. The third is another meaning that has been built up by images we have come to associate with a particular word. When this last meaning becomes strong enough, it takes over as the regular dictionary meaning. But long before that happens, this other meaning affects us whenever we read or hear the word.

Not so long ago it was all right to call someone a *capitalist*. Thirty years ago Oxford dictionaries said a capitalist is a person who uses capital in business and a lot of people do that. But now Karl Marx has won and people object to being called capitalists because they would feel accused of exploiting the people who work for them. The associated meaning of capitalist has taken over and capitalists prefer to be called industrialists.

Most of us are very happy to drink champagne, when we get the chance, but would not like to be accused of drinking *intoxicating liquor*. That is a perfectly accurate description of champagne but, thanks to psycholinguistics, it turns a pleasure into a vice. When, on the other hand, champagne is described, as it has been, as 'frivolity captured in a glass', we feel very good about it. The words we choose can attract or repel. Our ability to use this knowledge, as with many other things in this book, can be used to manipulate people, or it can be used to help and encourage them or to achieve our legitimate aims.

A nudist, even in the latest dictionaries, is someone who goes around naked because it is healthy. But no one wants to be called a nudist any more because the word connects up with exhibitionism and strip-tease shows. A BBC reporter has said *nude* rhymes with lewd, rude and crude. If you enjoy walking around naked, the in-word is *naturist* which has a nice comfortable feeling of living naturally and simply. No one cares if it makes all the rest of us unnaturists. With words it's every man for himself.

When James Callaghan was prime minister and Donald Coggan was Archbishop of Canterbury, the *Daily Telegraph* ran this headline on the front page:
CALLAGHAN 'TOO BUSY' TO HEAR COGGAN'S APPEAL
Almost every word is loaded with associated meanings. The unprefixed surnames diminish the stature of both men. When we say we are too busy, we usually mean we can't be bothered. And the headline writer made it worse by adding quotation marks—'too busy'. The word 'appeal' carries with it the suggestion of a request for help or mercy. We are left feeling that the prime minister couldn't be bothered to take time off to listen to a humanitarian request from the archbishop.

The negative meanings disappear when the headline is rewritten:
MR CALLAGHAN UNABLE TO MEET ARCHBISHOP
As the Goons used to say, it's all in the mind, which is what psycholinguistics is about.

This headline was unflattering to Michael Foot when he was leader of the Labour Party:
FOOT HANGS ON TO LEADERSHIP
It makes us think of someone hanging on to a cliff by his

fingertips. The unprefixed surname makes Mr Foot seem even more desperate. See what a different feeling this gives:

MICHAEL FOOT RETAINS LEADERSHIP

The Christian name and surname together are friendly. The word 'retains' gives a feeling of confidence and ability.

Even on the telephone maybe we should think twice before saying 'hang on', because it leaves someone out on a limb. 'I'll be back with you in a moment' is more encouraging. Perhaps it doesn't matter all that much, but it's worth being aware of the difference.

At the end of a letter quoted earlier, a girl wrote 'Please forgive me for not turning up for the appointment'. If you have ever been left waiting under a clocktower or in the foyer of a hotel, 'not turning up' echoes resentful memories. If she had written 'Please forgive me for being unable to keep our appointment' the other person might feel less negative about it.

Some words can affect our mood, our state of mind and even our physical state. When we are talking to someone, we are often aware we have said something that has upset them because there is a reaction or change of mood. This gives us a chance to put things right. But when we use the wrong words in a letter, we are not there to see the effect. I once saw a distinguished publisher hopping mad, waving about a letter and shouting 'What the hell does he mean writing to me like this?'

The letter was asking a favour and surely the writer had no idea it would get that reaction. He had used unintentionally, or at least without conscious intent, words with a powerful negative symbolism. It is easy to see what a mess psycholinguistics can make of things when we are using words to help someone or to ask someone to help us.

The following experiment has demonstrated how much words affect people. If you saw it carried out, you would always be on guard against certain words. The word HOPELESS is printed in large letters on a card or projected on to a screen and someone is asked to look at it for several minutes. The images associated with that word begin to take over and you see the person's face change. With some people, their pulse rate drops.

Other words like PATIENCE and COURAGE will

encourage a positive attitude. Word-therapy of this kind is used in some clinics. The large display of the word SILENCE in some libraries not only makes people speak in hushed voices, it can make them feel quiet and reflective.

This has been compared to colours in a room. In a room facing north, designers use pinks, reds and browns because they are 'warm' colours. Certain colours can make us feel low-spirited; others make us light-hearted. Tests have been carried out using two reception rooms with different colour schemes, letting visitors choose which room they wait in. The results show that people are strongly attracted to certain colours and put off by others. Like words, colours work on us as symbols and connect with feelings and experiences beyond our conscious recall.

Advertising agencies are aware that they have to find out how people react to words, pictures, colours and ideas. It is not enough just to ask them, because people will often respond to things in ways they themselves do not know about or understand.

When a new brand of sherry was being launched, regular sherry drinkers were shown three different labels. They put them in order of preference. The advertising agency was doubtful about the result and was advised by a psychologist to carry out a different test. This time the same sherry was put into three bottles with the different labels on them. People tasted a glass from each bottle and listed the sherries in order of quality. Hardly anyone said all three sherries were the same; there were marked preferences. When these were averaged out the result was not at all the same as the straight label test.

People may prefer certain colours and designs of labels, for one reason or another, but they associate other colours and designs with good sherry. If you are selling sherry, that's what counts. A brilliant designer might produce a beautiful label but if the associations are wrong, it would not sell sherry.

In another test, women were given a pat of butter and a pat of margarine to compare. The margarine was yellow and the butter was white. More than 90 per cent of the women picked out the yellow pat as butter. Because it is the colour of sunshine and buttercups, people associate yellow with freshly churned butter and the association is so strong that it had a stronger influence than the taste.

At one time margarine manufacturers worked hard and unsuccessfully to make us pronounce 'margarine' with a hard 'g', as in 'bargain'; they wanted to break away from the negative association of *marge*.

In the early days of instant coffee, advertisers got off to a bad start by stressing words such as 'quick', 'time-saving', 'efficient'. These are all words without warmth and feeling. Makers of fresh coffee fought back with warm happy words— 'aroma', 'flavour', 'rich', 'fresh'. Makers of instant coffee soon learned the lesson and changed to the warmest, most appetising words they could find.

It is futile to fight strong associations that exist in people's minds. Certain words and ideas make us react in a particular way, leave us more helpful or less helpful, move us towards something or pull us away from it. When we want to get through to people, we can use these forces to work for us.

Here is another way to understand this vital aspect of language. Next time you get a letter that affects your emotions to an extent that seems out of proportion to what has been said, spend a few minutes looking closely at the words. You might find out what has caused your mood and made you depressed, irritable or pleased with life.

Dr Jung believed that many of these feelings are part of our inheritance of the human condition, just as the human body has a long evolutionary history behind it. He called them *archetypes* and compared them to the impulse of birds to build nests, or ants to form organised colonies. Most of us know from our dreams that our unconscious is teeming with ideas and connections that can upset or disturb us at any moment, just as there are other associations that make us feel secure and comfortable. When on a bleak cold day we sit by a crackling log fire, it is not only the warmth that draws us but a deeply felt response to a symbol of security.

All this may seem remote and arcane when you are sitting down to write a letter, dictating to your secretary or picking up the telephone. But everyone who uses words successfully to sell, convince, inspire or comfort must develop an awareness of the feeling behind the meaning of words.

We need to be particularly careful when we are making or dealing with a complaint, because that is a situation where we can in a flash spark off resentment, fear or aggression. From then on, it is an uphill job to get something put right. We need not be conciliatory but it is wise to look at our words extra carefully. Otherwise we arouse a negative reaction that affects the way someone acts on our letter. Read these two letters written to a department store, complaining about a faulty electric toaster:

Letter 1
I am writing to complain about the electric toaster I bought from you only last week.
    No matter what I do with the regulator switch, the toast is always burnt.

The moment anyone reads 'I am writing to complain', the reaction is 'here comes trouble' and up come defences and resistance. If you want to, you can take it all the way back to childhood when we were afraid of being scolded or smacked for doing something wrong. If you think that is fanciful, check your own reaction next time someone picks up on you.

Letter 2
I thought how much you would like to know that the assistant who served me in your electrical department last week couldn't have been more helpful.
    In spite of that, though, there is something not right with the regulator on the toaster that I bought, because the toast keeps coming out burnt.

The woman who wrote that worked at avoiding negative reactions. She even wrote 'not right' instead of 'wrong'. The first letter produced a reply asking for the toaster to be brought in for repair. The second letter resulted in someone telephoning to say a new toaster was being sent and the other one would be collected at the same time.
    Words change the way we feel about things. An unofficial strike or lock-out sounds irresponsible and aggressive. For a while, everyone felt better when it was called 'industrial action' as that sounded more positive and disciplined. But by now the words 'industrial action' have lost their appeal. Good

words can turn sour if negative associations build up.

When the Writers' Guild of Great Britain advertised a charitable holiday retreat for writers, they wrote 'By the terms of the trust non-men are excluded'. In trying to avoid problems by excluding *non-men*, rather than women, they walked into a much worse-trap: non-men has a strong flavour of inadequacy like non-event and non-starter. Words get us into trouble if we are not alert to their symbolism.

On a BBC programme, Len Murray, then general secretary of the Trades Union Congress, said 'negotiations with the government are at an end'. For Denis Healey, a government minister at the time, it was 'a pause to let the dust settle'. They were both talking about the same breakdown in discussions.

No one knows how much disruption in our society at all levels is caused by the wrong words being used. Sometimes we can hear it going on. In a BBC news broadcast, industrial action by ASLEF, the train drivers' union, was described by a representative of British Rail as 'stupid unofficial action'. The editor of *The Sunday Times*, which had ceased publication because of a dispute with a union, called the union's attitude 'idiot logic'. Perhaps both statements were justified. What is certain is that words such as *stupid* and *idiot* arouse strong negative emotions and keep both sides away from the negotiating table.

It is worth looking very hard at some of the words we are in the habit of using, in case we have forgotten how they could affect other people. Because all of us relate to words. Some words make us feel good, other words make us feel bad. Publishers sell off cheaply unsold copies of books and call them publishers' remainders. But 'remainders' has an association of unappetising left-overs. Why not *publishers' offers*, which sounds generous and friendly? It is depressing to be an old age pensioner but you can hold your head up when you are called a *senior citizen*. It's charity when you apply for public assistance but *social security* is a right. And nobody wants the dole when they can get *unemployment benefit*.

The same things said in different ways can make people feel differently about them. At other times when descriptions are updated, something is lost. The Postmaster General sounds an approachable father-figure. The Chairman and Chief Executive of the Post Office Board (as he now is) seems distant and remote. Fortunately the attempt to call postmen *delivery officers* was thrown out by Parliament.

In a laboratory or Court of Law, precise definitions are essential. With people, it is more important for words to make them react positively. If the Chancellor of the Exchequer ever becomes the Chief Accountant it would, in our hearts, take something off the value of the pound.

Even simple price tags can be manipulated to get a better reaction. Those old drapery shopkeepers who put 2/11¾d or 99 cents on a price ticket knew what they were doing. It kept the price on the right side of the three shilling and one dollar barriers. The price ticket game still goes on but these days the stakes are much higher. Recently a new pocket television set was advertised 'for just £99.95', which keeps it on the right side of the hundred pound barrier.

Our reactions to these things are not logical. They are nonetheless real and affect our attitudes. If you have to keep someone waiting, perhaps it is better to say 'It will be ready in fifty-five minutes' instead of 'It will be ready in an hour'. We feel better if we have a month's holiday rather than four weeks; and would rather have a special price than a cut price. Humans are a compound of irrational feelings and logical intellect but our experiences of ourselves and our relationships with others show it is feelings that carry the day more often.

Games with words have a way of making us respond in a friendly way. Psychologists shy away from any attempt to analyse that indefinable, indispensable and apparently exclusively human attribute, a sense of humour. All we know is that when it is activated we feel cheerful.

Wordplay is often a form of punning and puns are usually derided. Yet Shakespeare, an undisputed master of language, enjoyed playing with words. When it is well done, wordplay can make us remember something or react sympathetically. Here are some nice examples:

GREEN SHIELD FORECASTS LESS STICKY TIMES
(The title of an article about how Green Shield stamps were trying to make a recovery with new incentive and promotion schemes.)

SCOTCH ON THE ROCKS
(The title of a piece by a city editor about the financial

problems of the Scotch whisky industry.)
                    Afjordable Norway
(From the Norwegian National Tourist Office about low price
holidays in Norway.)
        LAWSON SET FOR ANOTHER POUNDING
(The lead-in to an article on how the pressure on sterling was
making life difficult for Nigel Lawson, as Chancellor of the
Exchequer.)
            Stuff the bird! What about the Pudding?
(Advertising a Christmas pudding.)

Winston Churchill played with the *sound* of words. If you
listen to recordings of wartime speeches, you will hear him
pronounce Nazis as *Nahzies*, so they sound like the 'nasties' in
a children's fairy story, unpleasant, evil and to be overcome.

There are warm words and cold words, as there are warm
and cold colours. Warm words help us to feel secure and
comfortable. Cold words leave us uneasy, give us doubts or
put us completely against something. Cold words have their
place when the situation calls for them but we should always
be aware of the effect they may have on people.

We become more sensitive about using words when we start
to look at them in this way. To start you off, here are some
examples of warm and cold words which demonstrate how
psycholinguistics can help us to get through to others in the
way that we want to.

A few warm words:

Agree   When someone says 'I completely agree with you'
we get a warm glow. When something is agreeable, it is
pleasant. We like being agreeably surprised.

Basic   Something that is basic feels firm, solid and reliable.
A basic proposition or a basic idea suggests that it is founded
on sensible first principles.

Broad-based   A stage further than 'basic'. Something broad-
based is not going to topple easily. It is not just a flash in the
pan but sound and secure.

Care   A very comforting word. It is reassuring to be told
'We care very much about doing our best for you.' The phrase
'couldn't care less' is chilling.

Fair   Full of good associations. There is 'the fair sex', 'My
Fair Lady', 'None but the brave deserve the fair'. If something
is 'fair enough', we don't argue about it. Phrases such as 'It

seems fair to suggest', 'fair to ask', help to disarm argument.

If we have to back down over something and write or say 'It seems fair to agree', we may turn a negative into a positive.

Forward-looking It is human nature to be apprehensive about what might happen next. When we hear the words forward-looking we feel more secure, because someone has looked at least as far as the end of the road, even if not around the corner.

Good The word has the same origin as God and our warm response to it is archetypal.

Gratitude One of the warmest feelings one human being can have towards another.

Heart The heart is the pulse of life. It is a word that can move us when we read it or hear it used: 'with all my heart', 'heartfelt', 'Your letter gives me much heart'.

Hope An old Anglo-Saxon word. It is almost impossible to keep going without hope. Dante chose appropriate words for the doors of hell: 'All hope abandon, ye who enter here'.

When there is nothing else you can say in a situation at least use the word *hope*. It keeps the door open.

Independent It carries with it a warm feeling of being unbiased, open-minded, objective, free. It was good psycholinguistics to call the alternative television service *independent television* instead of 'commercial television'. (See *commercial* in the list of cold words.)

Love A marvellous word to use when you can. Even when things are as drab as can be, it is a word that can make life still worth living. Perhaps it is the warmest word in the language.

New Paradoxically one of the very old words in English, going back beyond Anglo-Saxon to Old Norse. Although it has been used so much in advertising, research continues to show that *new* still has a lot of life left in it. Dr Ernest Dichter, the motivational research psychologist, urged copywriters to use *new* in their headlines whenever possible.

Simplicity John Tessimond, the poet who was an advertising copywriter wrote:

One day people will touch and talk perhaps easily,
And loving be natural as breathing and warm as sunlight,
And people will untie themselves, as string is unknotted,

Unfold and yawn and stretch and spread their fingers,
Unfurl, uncurl like seaweed returned to the sea,
And work will be simple and swift as a seagull flying,
And play will be casual and quiet as a seagull settling,
And the clocks will stop, and no one will wonder or care
    or notice,
And people will smile without reason, even in the winter,
    even in the rain.

Most of us yearn for a life free from complications, which is why *simplicity* is such a very warm word.

Sincere A reader just glosses over 'Yours sincerely' at the end of a letter. But a sentence that begins 'I sincerely believe . . .' could make us read it in a different way.

Special Everyone feels someone special. So we all like the idea of getting special attention or special consideration. It is a word we still pay attention to, even if we do get too many 'special offers'.

Young It goes back to Anglo-Saxon so it has been in the language a long time. But it remains lively, with echoes of spring, freshness and enthusiasm.

Cold words are words in the shadow. Politicians often use them about opposition parties. There are times when we have to use words like these but we should not use them unnecessarily.

A few cold words:

Abnormal A sinister word that makes people uneasy.

Afraid A word that goes with darkness and gloom. It is often used when it could be avoided:

I'm afraid it will be another five minutes . . .
We are afraid that we cannot accept your order without payment in advance . . .
I'm afraid he can't see you at the moment . . .

Of course it is just a manner of speaking but why link up with a negative emotion when you could say:

Just five minutes and it will be all ready . . .
We look forward to dealing with your order, although

please send payment in advance . . .
I'm sorry he's engaged at the moment . . .

But   This little word is double-edged. It can put people on guard or it can encourage them. If you say 'It's very good but . . .', your *but* will produce an immediate reaction of caution. If you say 'It will be very difficult but . . .', your *but* gives hope. It is a word to watch. Be especially careful of 'Yes, but . . .' 'Although' is a useful word to substitute.

Cannot   Look at these sentences from actual letters:

We cannot deliver in three weeks . . .
I cannot get it done for you . . .

Cannot   is a rejecting word which leaves the other person out in the cold. You can get a better reaction occasionally by avoiding it:

Can you give us five weeks for delivery . . . ?
I'm sorry it's not possible to do it . . .

Cash in   It has a strong flavour of opportunism. Be careful about telling someone they are cashing in on a situation, unless you mean to attack them. On the other hand, it's all right to 'make the most' of anything. Same man—different hat.

Commercial   Of course this word has a perfectly harmless and legitimate use, but sometimes carries with it the suggestion of being more interested in profits than quality and integrity— 'the commercial theatre', 'too commercial'. It is a word to watch.

Disappoint   When we write or say 'I'm sorry to disappoint you . . .', we are inviting people to feel more disappointed than they might have been.

Disagree   Look at the other person's face when you say, 'I disagree with you'. There will nearly always be a defensive reaction. This happens very often at meetings and a lot of time and energy are wasted. These other ways have been used to side-step a conflict:

Can we look at it another way?
Would you consider another point of view?
Here's something else worth looking at.

Dislike   Another rejecting word that should be used only if you do not want to be warmer and more friendly.

Doubt   Most people have doubts about many things. Why remind them and make them hesitate? You could change 'Although you may have some doubts' to 'Although you may want to consider this'.

Risk   The word often makes people react irrationally. Lord Rothschild, in a lecture he called *Risk*, said there is no such thing as a risk-free society. He quoted an old Chinese proverb to show that even a simple life has risk: 'The couple who go to bed early to save candles end up with twins.'

What matters is the degree of risk. Is it one in a million or one in ten? When people read or hear the word *risk*, they often don't ask that question, so we risk putting them off.

Unfair and *Unreasonable*   Both are words of accusation and nearly always produce a strong defensive attitude in return. Be careful about using them, unless you want a fight.

Unfortunately   A depressing word often used unnecessarily:

Unfortunately we weren't able to get in touch with you . . .
Unfortunately we cannot accept it . . .
Unfortunately the price is too high . . .

As a result, a negative statement becomes even more negative. There are many more warm and cold words. When you get into the habit of looking at the emotional colouring of words, as well as at their meanings, you will find yourself using more good words and avoiding off-putting ones, unless there is no other way.

Face to face

An encounter between two people is always a little strange and mysterious because there are so many psychic reactions: shyness, fears, anxieties, memories, dreams, longings, fill the space between us and another person.

The same forces make our communications successful whether we are faxing a letter to a company on the other side of the world, shouting to a man on the other side of the road or speaking in bed to someone we love. We always have to get their attention, keep their interest and relate to them as one human being to another.

But when we send a letter, words are everything. Take them away and all that is left is a blank sheet of paper or just a letter-heading. When we are speaking to someone face to face, words are only part of the communication between us. Take them away and all kinds of messages still pass across.

Peter Brook, the theatre producer, uses experiments in communication without words. He asks actors to express feelings and thoughts by using their eyes or the back of the head or just by movement of the torso, keeping the arms and legs still. In an actors' studio in New York, I saw a girl express what she was feeling by nothing more than coming into the room and sitting down. Although nothing was said, a remarkably clear message came through.

Dr David Mendel, a former cardiologist at St Thomas's Hospital in London, believes doctors should learn to read patients' faces to help with diagnosis. He says that even when a patient is silent:

> His face is talking and may sometimes be wildly signalling . . . When he listens to the doctor, the reception of each word is registered on his face and if the doctor ignores this running commentary on his 'spiel', he is a fool.

If you turn off the sound on a television set, you still understand a lot of what is going on. Sydney Newman, the Canadian producer who did so much to develop television drama in the early days, tells us:

> I well remember getting fed up to the teeth telling good radio and stage writers that to learn how to write for the camera, they should imagine that all their characters are 90 per cent mute.

Until it is demonstrated to them, most people think that when they are face to face with someone, they have to use words in the same way as when writing letters or reports. At interviews and meetings, if you expect words to do the whole job of communication, you will probably use far too many words, which dilutes their effect.

Sitting opposite someone, you need less words because your face and body help to convey your meaning and so does the way you speak. The other person unconsciously expects this because he is looking and listening instead of reading. If you sit without movement or expression and talk in a flat voice, communication is at half cock.

There is no need, of course, to wave our arms about and give a performance. That would be distracting. But it is important to be aware how we can help our words work harder when we are talking directly to someone. Small things can have a big effect.

Leaning forward in your chair can underline the sincerity of what you are saying. Looking away and then looking back at the other person can make words seem more considered. A smile can turn a simple 'thank you' into an expression of deep gratitude. Putting a hand on someone's shoulder and looking into their eyes can say all the words in our heart at that moment.

These are only examples because what is natural for one person is not appropriate for another. All of us have to find the gestures and expressions that come naturally. A woman uses different ones from a man. What is effective for a man of fifty can be all wrong for someone of twenty-five and, more important still, the other way round.

Our age, our style and the situation all affect the ways we can help our words to get through successfully at meetings and interviews. Some people find they communicate much more effectively just by saying less. These things are personal and individual and cannot be forced; but as we become more aware of the possibilities, our own style can develop.

When we are talking to someone, their attention is not focussed in the same way as when they are reading a letter. An encounter between two people is always a little strange and mysterious because there are so many psychic reactions: shyness, fears, anxieties, memories, dreams, longings, fill the space between us and another person.

If it is someone we know, all the circumstances of our relationship are touched. Status often gets in the way, too often, and then nobody thinks straight or talks straight because they are too conscious of their own position or of someone else's. With a stranger, there are all the associations of type, looks, age, personality and sex.

We may appear to have a captive audience because someone is there listening. But their thoughts are not captive and they could be all over the place. Shorter sentences, simpler words and straightforward turns of phrase stand a much better chance of getting through successfully.

Speaking slowly encourages someone to take us seriously, although if you speak too slowly people can lose the sense, or go to sleep. Speaking too fast usually transmits nervousness and uncertainty to the other person. An experienced actress passed on this advice to a young colleague: 'As I feel my heart beating faster, I concentrate on talking slowly and my nervousness goes or at least it doesn't run away with me.'

If you are nervous at an interview or making a presentation, you are in good company, because people at the top feel the same way. As she was facing her maiden General Election in 1979, Margaret Thatcher told us ' . . . when you're terribly nervous, your voice does tend to rise and the cure is to try to be more relaxed . . . You're frightened to death but never mind!' Of course Mrs Thatcher has gained so much more confidence since those days, although perhaps something has been lost on the way, as overconfidence can lead to oversell. As with so many things in life, the right balance is all.

There is no point in shouting and it is always more difficult to understand words when they are being said too loud. A successful chief executive in America has the habit of saying, in the midst of a heated meeting, 'Not so loud please. I can't hear you.'

The most common fault in face to face communication is saying too much too quickly. You can re-read a letter if you don't understand something but you cannot re-read an interview. If a letter is too long, you can pick out the points that matter: if someone talks too much, the wood disappears among the trees.

We can draft and re-draft an important letter as often as we like. But a meeting or interview is a one-night stand and we cannot write the whole script in advance. How do we find the words we need when there's no time to think about them? The best advice is to go back to the basic principle of all good communication. Make sure you know precisely what result you want and keep your attention on that. Then the words you say will lead in the direction you want to go, which is much more important than saying something clever.

When we convince people, reassure them or comfort them, we do not use clever words. Clever words are for parliamentary arguments, debating societies and TV quiz-shows. In most other situations there is a natural suspicion of over persuasiveness. Oversell puts people off; you see them walking away in the marketplace when a salesman puts on too much pressure.

With someone we care about, simplicity is all. After a long talk with her father, a daughter wrote:

'Talk is cheap', they say, and some talk is undoubtedly cheap. But one is alone in the end with one's problems and unhappiness, and the words of another can be just enough to keep one going on and trying once again. That is what your words bring me.

Not clever words but only a simple expression of our common humanity can do what that girl described.

The president of one of the great Oxford colleges is a surprisingly quiet and gentle man, who nevertheless has to control meetings of the governing body. He gave this as his secret:

When it is something very important, I try not to sound too serious about it, because that makes everyone put on their thinking-caps. When you make something sound too important, people are afraid to make a decision. So when I can, I try to make sure that my voice is lighthearted, almost nonchalant.

His advice is a warning of what can happen if we are too intense. But we can be too relaxed, overanxious to put ourselves or the other person at ease. Then time is often wasted and the real business has to be rushed.

The broadcaster, David Jacobs, was for many years chairman of the weekly BBC programmes *Any Questions* and *Any Answers*. There is a different panel each week, so he was always meeting new people. For the first minute or so he used to make 'social sounds', as he called them, to help his guests relax: 'Did you get here easily?', 'Have any trouble parking?', 'Did you come up from London?' and so on. But he would not allow this to go on for more than a short while or it would detract from the purpose and meaning of the encounter.

Even the way we set up a meeting can help. A producer telephoned an impresario:

> *Producer* : Can you spare me fifteen minutes of your time?
> The impresario agreed, suggested a day and asked what time would be convenient.
> *Producer* : What time do you leave for home?
> '6.45' came the answer.
> *Producer* : If it's all right with you, I'll come at 6.15.

The other man would be more relaxed because the day's work was done. He would know the meeting wouldn't drag on and that the point would be reached quickly.

In someone else's office, we are at a disadvantage because it's another man's territory. But the other man can help. The producer recalled with warmth how the impresario got up from behind his desk and came forward to meet him.

It is a great opportunity to talk to someone face to face. You have an advantage you can never have with a letter. A letter goes out blind; you're not there to see how the other person reacts and the best you can do is to anticipate hang-ups and doubts. When someone is in front of you, there is a chance to spot a misunderstanding and put it right before it becomes a block. You can see when a point needs making again. If you are helping someone, you can give comfort and encouragement the moment you see anxiety and fear.

All that is lost if we think only of ourselves and what we are saying. When we are carried away by what we want to say, the other person usually gets left behind.

As we have seen, famous and successful people can be

nervous at face to face encounters, no matter how well they cover it up. Other people avoid them at times and prefer to write letters instead, thereby missing valuable opportunities. It helps to think of an interview or a meeting with someone as the greatest chance in the world for real communication, because that's what it is. We usually get through more successfully when we try to be ourselves. Here is Margaret Thatcher, again on the eve of her first General Election: 'I am what I am and I will stay that way. I just hope to improve in communication as I go along.' In those early days at least, her heart was in the right place.

When you talk to someone from behind a desk, that lump of teak or mahogany between you can be a real barrier, if you let it, and interfere with good face to face communication, just as a platform or a microphone can separate speakers from their audience. In David Jacobs' home in London I saw a message, finely engraved in italic script, from the late Ed Murrow, an outstanding American broadcaster:

> The fact that your voice is amplified to the degree where it reaches from one end of the country to the other does not confer upon you greater wisdom and understanding than you possessed when your voice reached only from one end of the bar to the other.

David Jacobs, who spends a lot of his time in front of a microphone, hung that message where he couldn't miss it, just behind the lavatory.

When to keep quiet

We have largely forgotten silence. It even embarrasses us; we clap our hands mechanically because we do not know what else to do, and we are unaware that silence is also permitted, that silence is also good.
Peter Brook, *The Empty Space*

Words can work wonders but there are times when we should hold them back, when the result we want comes through saying less or perhaps nothing at all. The best way to deal with some letters is not to reply to them.

In the hardest, toughest negotiations a knowledge of when to keep quiet can lead to success. If you doubt that, think back to the last time you came out of a meeting or an interview or hung up the telephone and were left with an uneasy feeling that you had said too much. Take heart if that has ever happened to you because it has happened to nearly everyone. It was reported that Joe Haines, former press secretary to Sir Harold Wilson, believed that during the October 1974 election his boss appeared on television too often. Anyone can make the mistake of saying too much.

We are so accustomed to noise, verbiage, instant comment on everything that we seriously undervalue silence. There are many practical situations in which things go better for us, or we help someone else much more, simply by keeping quiet. Here are six cases, as always in this book, taken from real life:

The Service Manager

The service manager in a big garage was looking for a way to increase productivity by changing the system of workflow. He called in his three best fitters to get ideas.

He explained the problem and then gave his own solution in some detail. When he asked for suggestions nothing much came forth and he was left with his own ideas.

Some time afterwards he learned that the other men did not see much point in thinking too hard about the problem, because he had already come up with a solution and they were reluctant to cut across that. He said it was a lesson to him in when to shut up.

If we are trying to get someone's ideas about anything, from a production control system to how to repair our washing-machine, we should be careful about rushing in with our own suggestions. Peter Brook tells us that no theatre director, whatever his capabilities, can understand a character in the same way as an actor who is actually playing the part:

> . . . one has to be very careful in the early stages not to trample on any fragile and instinctive buds that are sprouting.

137

Keeping quiet often creates an expectant atmosphere that encourages other people's ideas to come to the surface.

The Social Worker

Kathy, a social worker, was troubled about a particular family in her area. It was difficult because she never had the chance to talk to any one of them on their own, until one day she found Susan, the seventeen-year-old daughter, at home alone. Kathy seized the opportunity to ask some questions.

Susan was slow to reply and Kathy tried to help her by suggesting possible answers. The meeting did not lead anywhere. Later on, Kathy saw that she had not given Susan time to feel trust and confidence and she wished she had just waited quietly for answers to her questions.

Some clever and sensitive people ponder on problems and are often diffident about coming up with their own opinion, especially if another suggestion has been made. Others will try to say something different, even if they agree with a point of view, because they feel it is expected of them or they want to assert themselves. When we see someone is thinking and trying to make the right connections, it is better to wait quietly instead of interfering with the process by talking.

It's the same the other way round. If you are the one who has to come up with an answer, be prepared to wait until you are ready. Our society puts a premium on quick thinking but it also values measured consideration. You can take your choice. Most people respond to someone saying 'Would you mind if I think about this for a few minutes?' There is a solicitor who politely offers a client a magazine to look at until he is ready with an answer to their question.

On radio and television it is always a rapid fire of questions and answers because there is no time to wait. But you have only to listen to the voices to know that these are contests of wit, not a search for wisdom and understanding. Sometimes the only honest answer to that overanxious question 'Well, what do you think?' is 'I'm still thinking'.

The Secretary in the Ad Agency

Rosalind wanted a chance to be a copywriter. She tried her hand at writing advertisements and thought she had some good ideas. The next thing was to take them along to the creative director.

As he started reading what she had written, she explained why she had put certain things in and left others out, the purpose of the copy, whom it was aimed at and what other ideas she had discarded.

He put up with this for a while, then stopped reading and looked up:

> It's better, Rosalind, either to write something down and let the other person read it. Or go along and tell them about it. But you have to choose. Otherwise who knows whether to listen or read? I've been trying to do both and not making a good job of either.

It is very common to ask someone to read a letter or a report, or to examine something, and to talk to them while they are doing it. We are often afraid not to fill the air with words even if those words get in the way. Insecurity and uncertainty, the most universal of all human feelings, make us say too much and write too much. We all need to justify ourselves. Yet time and again talking too much about our work and our ideas brings unnecessary doubts to the surface. There are usually doubts about most things and it is often better not to stir them up.

Thor Heyerdahl says this about doubts, and he should know, having drifted from South America to Polynesia on the Kon-Tiki raft and then, later on, sailing across the Indian Ocean on a boat made out of reeds:

> There have been moments in my life when, if I had a mere second of doubt, I would never have done what I did. But if you believe something, you can do it. The problem is to believe it.

There is no need to add to that problem by saying too much.

The Personnel Director

Management and union were negotiating on a productivity deal. The personnel director discovered the shop steward had made a significant error in the calculations he had presented. He sent for him, showed him where he had slipped up and pointed out that such an error was irresponsible because it could cause serious disruption in industrial relations.

When the shop steward left the office, the personnel director had a nice feeling of self-satisfaction. But it didn't last very long. Within a few weeks there was an unofficial strike over some minor matter.

If someone makes a mistake there can be an almost irresistible urge to rub their nose in it. If we give way to that we often pay later on. It is a rule of human nature that when we make people feel inferior they have an instinctive drive to compensate. 'Be nice to people on your way up', the wise old statesman advised, 'as you might meet them on your way down.' If that is too cynical and self-seeking for you, there is another way to see it: generosity is one of the warmest of all human qualities. We have to tell people when things are wrong but we can choose to say it in as few words as possible.

The TV Writer

She had submitted an idea for a TV series to the head of a big television company in Los Angeles. As she explained it, she could see he was interested, especially when he began to talk to her about the things he liked.

This encouraged her to go on building it up still further. Then she noticed that the curve of his enthusiasm was starting to turn downwards. Luckily she stopped in time. The TV series was made but she was convinced that if she had not kept quiet at that moment the idea might have been shelved.

In almost any discussion, when one person is trying to convince another, there is a peak. It is marked sometimes by the other person beginning to talk almost as if it is *their* idea. That's the moment to keep quiet, because after a peak the next direction must be downwards.

The Interviewer

Not one interviewer in particular but all those interviewers on television and radio who come between us and someone we want to listen to, which happens when the interviewer does most of the talking. An angry television critic wrote once 'Television interviewers should be neither seen nor heard.'

Every time we catch ourselves interrupting someone it is a warning that we are probably not getting as much out of the conversation as we might be.

TV advertising time costs so much that some advertisers are afraid not to stuff every second with words. 'Many words lead to exhaustion' Lao Tzu, the Chinese prophet, said. When we watch TV that's what it feels like sometimes and we yearn for a pause in the soundtrack.

The absence of sound can have a powerful effect. There is an American public service commercial to counteract drug abuse which does not use a single word. During thirty seconds of silence we watched an addict giving himself a fix. The effect is chilling and the warning against drug addiction more powerful than any words.

There are different ways of keeping quiet. Silence can be respectful or sympathetic or compassionate. We can be quiet because we want to give the other person a chance, or our silence can be morose or sullen and aggressive. When silence is directed at offering help and understanding, it can only enrich a meeting. Macaulay, the 19th century writer and politician, was said to have 'occasional flashes of silence that make his conversation perfectly delightful'. Thomas Hardy said of someone, 'That man's silence is wonderful to listen to.' Of the theatre, Peter Brook says:

> We have largely forgotten silence. It even embarrasses us; we clap our hands mechanically because we do not know what else to do, and we are unaware that silence is also permitted, that silence is also good.

The theatre, at its best, is a concentrated interpretation of real life and great actors on stage are masters of communication. The actor, John Gielgud, passed on an important lesson when he advised that 'Pauses are as important as speech'.

In broadcasting, Terry Wogan has been called the best exponent of the 'creative pause'. If a celebrity tries to upstage him by a clever remark on his chat show, Wogan has a way of waiting for what seems a long time before replying. Everyone waits for his next word. Wogan may look up thoughtfully, smile and say in disarming mock-admiration 'Gosh!' The audience fall about. When we time our pauses well, everyone will pay close attention to what we say next.

I know a composer who became a millionaire because most of his compositions were jingles for TV commercials. He lived in a world of tinkling pianos, tape-recorders and vocal groups. Once when he asked me a question there must have been a pause for all of five seconds while I thought about the answer. 'What's the matter?' he demanded in a panic, 'I can't stand these terrible silences!'

Dag Hammarskjold, as secretary general of the United Nations, was surrounded by talk but believed it was a waste of human resources ' . . . to talk merely because convention forbids silence'. He designed an oasis of silence for the UN headquarters in New York, a room to be quiet in for anyone who works at the UN or visits it. Silence is an essential part of human relationships and the real quality of understanding between one person and another can be measured by the unspoken communication between them.

Here is a story of two people getting through to each other without words. It is told by John Georgiadis, leader of the London Symphony Orchestra, about the gala occasion to mark the ninetieth birthday of the conductor, Leopold Stokowski:

> The soloist that evening was a very beautiful Rumanian violinist. As we took our seats for dinner, there was a mild commotion at Number One Table.
>
> 'Why is the soloist sitting at Table Number Two?' a commanding voice was heard to say. 'I want her to sit opposite me at this table.'
>
> The distance between the soloist and the conductor was reduced, but conversation wasn't easy with the noise of a hundred people eating and drinking.
>
> Stokowski wrote something on his programme and passed it across the table to the soloist. She was confounded by the sight of one large solitary question mark.
>
> She sent back her reply, from a girl of twenty to a magnificent man of ninety—an exclamation mark.

A psychotherapist, who is warm and compassionate, says that she tries to allow herself what she calls the 'luxury and confidence of silence', when she is asked for advice about a difficult personal situation. She finds that by leaving the question hanging in mid-air, the other person will sometimes see for themselves the only possible answer to their dilemma.

A marriage guidance counsellor has observed that most

rows in families are caused by what someone says and that a row can often be prevented by listening rather than talking. But she adds that there is an all-important difference between listening and 'not answering'. Only if the feeling is right, does silence have a creative quality.

It is in the deepest of emotional experiences that words seem most out of place. Russell heard that his closest friend had been killed in a car crash. He went at once to Sophie, his friend's wife. When she opened the door, they went together into the kitchen and he sat with her, holding her hand for half an hour. Then he left. During his visit, nothing was said but years later Sophie still remembered the comfort and sympathy that came across.

A mother and daughter had not seen each other for three years and during that time there had been joy and sorrow in both their lives. When they met in the arrivals lounge at Kennedy Airport, the mother put her hands on her daughter's shoulders and held them firmly for what seemed a long time. Only then did they embrace and talk to each other. The daughter said she would remember that greeting for the rest of her life.

The culture and pressures of our society encourage and in fact demand that we describe, discuss and pass instant verbal judgement on everything. The concept of the ineffable is unwelcome, because unless we can talk about something, we are inarticulate, ineffective and no use at all on a television programme. Yet the compulsive need to say something about everything can come between us and real feeling. The quality of response to art, music or to any experience can suffer if we feel an overriding obligation to talk about it right away.

Some letters are best answered by silence. An angry, vituperative letter has often done its job for the writer by letting the poison out of their system. There are other letters, described by the editor of the Writer's Guild journal as 'written in pure adrenalin'. Most of us have second thoughts and don't post them. If you receive one and are trying to think about how to reply, consider the alternative of not replying. We do no good, and might do harm to ourselves, by replying to letters of that kind. If anyone should feel uneasy about not writing back, remember that silence has its own living quality and can have dignity, poise and courage.

We need words all the same to persuade, inform, comfort, encourage and to put our case to the next person. Words are the driving force of communication. Words get things done and that's what this book is all about. But though words can do so much for us, it is an important and valuable talent to know when *not* to use them.

Good and bad English

Grammar to a writer is a total irrelevance. If I start thinking about grammar, I get caught up in the how *instead of the* what . . . *grammar is a stranglehold on passion!*
Bernice Rubens, The Critics, BBC

The purpose of this chapter is to open up possibilities of using the English language in more relaxed, lively and expressive ways.

English is changing faster than at any time in its long history, changing under technological, geographical and social pressures. Many of the old arguments about what is good and bad English are becoming as outworn as pince-nez, wing-collars and high-button boots. Yet almost any of us can feel restricted at times in the use of the language, because we are uncertain where the boundaries are. Of course grammar still has a place but it should not come between us and what we want to say. When it gets in the way of good sense, grammar should give way and let us move freely and easily among the words and sentences of the most successful language in the world. For we cannot make good use of words if we have too many hang-ups about them.

When we use words naturally, they communicate better. If we strain to make our English absolutely 'correct', it is no guarantee that we shall get through to people. Over a hundred years ago, Henry Alford wrote a book called *The Queen's English*; it was Queen Victoria of course. His style is old-fashioned but his advice is as fresh as new paint:

> Aim at satisfying the common sense of those who read and hear, and then, though any one who has no better employment may pick holes in every third sentence, you will have written better English than one who suffers the tyranny of small critics to cramp the expression of his thoughts.

For far too long English was in the frigid grip of Latin and Greek scholars who made the running. Even by 1870, the study of English, as English, didn't count for much. There were no professors of modern English at Oxford or Cambridge; at Eton the English teacher came below the teacher of French and at Marlborough behind the dancing master. All grammar was based on Latin and Ancient Greek, perfect languages for grammarians because they are dead languages and the rules can be fossilised.

This is the source of tired old commandments such as:

Never begin a sentence with the conjunctions *and* or *but*.
Never end a sentence with the prepositions *with, on, to* or
for.
Never ever split an infinitive even if you have to turn a
double-somersault to avoid it.

The Authorised Version of the Bible, published in 1611 and
translated by forty-seven of the best scholars at the time,
begins:

In the beginning God created the heaven and the earth.
And the earth was without form and void; and darkness
was upon the face of the deep. And the spirit of God
moved upon the face of the waters. And God said, 'Let
there be light': and there was light. And God called the
light day, and the darkness he called night. And the
evening and the morning were the first day.

After that, need we worry about beginning a sentence, a
paragraph or even a chapter (as Charles Dickens did) with
that old Anglo-Saxon word *And?* Yet only recently a copywriter agency had a battle with a client who insisted it was
wrong.
The copywriter gave in because the next battle was more
important. He had written:

There are a lot of extras you don't have to pay for.

The client said you can't end a sentence with a preposition
and changed it to:

There are a lot of extras for which you don't have to
pay.

The copywriter asked the agency's research department for
help. 90 per cent of the people who were shown both sentences
said the client's version sounded unnatural and they had to
think about it. The client backed down.
There are two ways to look at English. One view is that
there is (or should be) a fixed grammar with definite
unchanging rules: the other view is that the rules of our
language are, at the last judgement, dependent on usage, on
how English is used by most people in writing and speaking.

Even good scholars get mixed up about this. H. W. Fowler, who wrote the classic *Modern English Usage*, is sometimes treated like the judge in a linguistic supreme court. Yet he refused 'to assume autocratic control of the language, and put to death all the words and phrases that do not enjoy our approval'.

That is open-minded. But the same man proclaimed 'Americanisms are foreign words and should be so treated.' Yet where would the English language be without gatecrasher, debunk, teenager, bulldoze, babysitter, crank, bluff, boom, slump, stunt, paperback and thousands of other indispensable 'Americanisms'. And what substitutes are there for the refreshingly simple NASA vocabulary of space travel, where *spacemen* wearing *spacesuits* are *blasted-off* in a *spaceship*?

A professor from London University and a professor from Princeton agree that 'The two varieties of English have never been so different as people have imagined, and the dominant tendency, for several decades now, has clearly been that of convergence and even greater similarity'.

All the evidence shows that English will never let itself be bossed about by anyone for long. The Society for Pure English, started in 1913 to guide the use and development of the English language, is as dead as a doornail. The Advisory Committee on Spoken English, set up by the BBC in 1926, with Bernard Shaw, Robert Bridges (the poet laureate), Julian Huxley and a young journalist called Alistair Cooke as members, threw in the towel in 1926. Lord Reith, then head of the BBC, spoke its epitaph: 'There are no experts, only users.'

If there are enough of us, the way we use English will drive a coach and horses through any set of rules that any professor of English lays down. All of us who use the language help to make it. As in many things in life, the people to listen to are the doers rather than the teachers.

Helped by his stint on the BBC advisory committee, Alistair Cooke made up his mind: 'Syntax may go to hell', he declared, 'so long as I sound like one man talking to another.' Bernice Rubens, the first woman to win the Booker Prize (in 1969 for her novel *The Elected Member*), has the same idea:

Grammar to a writer is a total irrelevance. If I start thinking about grammar, I get caught up in the *how* instead of the *what* . . . grammar is a stranglehold on passion.

She added this in a note to me:

> But before a writer discards grammar, he must know it intimately. He must at one time have loved it. He must *always* respect it. Only then is its irrelevance clear and logical.

John Salmon, as creative director of Collet, Dickenson, Pearce, a London advertising agency famous for winning creative awards, had this view about grammar:

> I only think about grammar if I am reading some copy and something brings me to a halt. It might be the grammar that sounds wrong or a peculiar word or just a clumsy sentence.

Carlos Slienger, an American-Mexican publisher and writer on political economy, shrugged when I asked him about grammar:

> Language is by definition functional. I never think about grammar as I am more interested in the flow of ideas. If someone says to me 'That's bad grammar' I reply 'Oh sure!'

There is a familiar anecdote about Winston Churchill's attitude towards stereotyped grammatical rules. When someone clumsily avoided ending a sentence with a preposition, Churchill is alleged to have written in the margin 'This is the short of muddled-up English up with which I will not put!'

Even Noah Webster, who recorded every word he could find in his great *American Dictionary of the English Language*, admitted:

> Language is like the course of the Mississippi, the motion of which is at times scarcely perceptible yet even then it possesses a momentum quite irresistible. Words and expressions will be forced into use in spite of all the exertions of all the writers in the world.

Yet somehow it does not become a free-for-all. English has to have a structure or it would become sloppy. Many people feel a responsibility towards this. Capital Radio, the independent radio station for London, has a lot of influence on the way English is used. 'Certain things drive me bananas'. John Whitney said to me, when he was managing director. 'If for example, announcers say *excetera* for etcetera or *garridge* for garage, I get someone to mention it to them. Why should we teach half London to pronounce words wrongly?'

All good writers and speakers play a part in keeping the structure of English in place but it is a light framework supporting the language, not heavy chains that shackle it. About this, there can be no more authoritative voice than Sir James Murray's, that stern bearded Victorian, first editor of *The Oxford English Dictionary*:

> . . . there is absolutely no defining line in any direction: the circle of English has a well-defined centre but no discernible circumference.

There is freedom in the way we can use English; there is also some order. The balance between the two is shifting and no one can lay it down for all time and for everyone.

In some dictionaries English words are divided into four categories.

Standard English   Words that are used even in the most formal situations.

Colloquial   (usually abbreviated *colloq.*)   Words used in everyday speech. Many are used in writing and in formal speech so it is hard to distinguish them from standard English.

The BBC, who give a lot of thought to language, use in official news bulletins *pub, shambles, phone, boss* and many other words that dictionaries may still list as *colloq.* or informal.

Slang   (usually abbreviated *sl.*)   These are words less generally acceptable, at least in writing, although most of them are understood by everyone. Some people never use them, even in their relaxed moments, and this can make their conversation and letters seem heavy-going.

Vulgar   (usually abbreviated *vulg.*)   Words that make your maiden aunt and a lot of other people blush. The notorious four-letter words come into this category.

According to the COD* these words are 'used only by those who have no wish to be thought polite or educated'. That's a slap in the face for the BBC, a number of leading novelists on both sides of the Atlantic, including at least one Nobel Prizewinner for Literature, many critics and journalists, some good poets such as W. H. Auden and Philip Larkin, me and perhaps you too.

The lines dividing these categories keep moving. *Colloq.* today becomes standard tomorrow. This year's *sl.* moves up to *colloq.* next year. The latest COD shows *upbeat* and *downbeat* as good standard words although they are not even listed (apart from reference to a musical term) in the much larger 1959 *Shorter Oxford English Dictionary. Up the spout* is standard but *up the creek* is slang. *To make a hash of something* is standard although if you *settle someone's hash* you're colloquial.

As for all those *vulg.* words, there is not much you can find on the walls of public loos (*colloq.*) that you cannot also read in serious novels and poetry and hear in theatres in Shaftesbury Avenue and on Broadway.

We need dictionaries and can all be grateful to those who slog away at compiling them. They help us find our way through the jungle of words. But many things, even in the best dictionary, can be no more than the opinion of the editor.

Just as so many old-established traditions in society are on the blink (*sl.*) so is the use of English. Words are changing their meanings and their status faster than ever before. 'After two months of uninterrupted intercourse', wrote Elizabeth Barrett Browning on her honeymoon in 1846, 'he loves me better every day . . . and my health improves too.' She would hardly write that now!

Nor can we call slang bad English. G. K. Chesterton said it is 'the one stream of poetry that is constantly flowing'. Carl Sandburg, the American poet born in Illinois, wrote:

Slang is language which takes off its coat,
Spits on its hands and goes to work.

If we want our words to do that, it is up to us to decide what words turn people on (*sl.*) and do the job we want. At a board meeting of a well known public company the chief

*COD - *The Concise Oxford Dictionary*, 1982 edition (1988 reprint). References from here on to standard, colloquial and slang are the opinions of that dictionary.

executive used deliberately the most notorious of all four-letter words to cut through the veneer of politeness that was holding up progress.

English can be all things to all people in their drive to express what they think and feel. Shakespeare twisted and stretched words to make them do what he wanted. Three hundred years later the American writer, Damon Runyon, invented Runyonese out of slang used by Brooklyn crooks.

In the 1890s someone came out with the vivid word *skyscraper* to describe the tall buildings going up in New York. In the 1960s John Lennon played around with words to arrive at *The Beatles*, the most memorable name of all for a pop group.

Editors of recent dictionaries acknowledge that spoken English is more and more influential and is lubricating the wheels of the written language, leaving it more easygoing. If you make sausages and want to call your product *The Posh Sausage*, go ahead. One manufacturer did and it looked good on posters.

If our words are not understood or are unsuitable at the time, in the place or the situation, they are bad English, because they are not getting through. When Edward Heath was prime minister his speech writers gave him a list of 'words to avoid, because they are meaningless to the majority of the audience'. In that context, they would have been bad English.

It is bad English to ask the waitress in a transport café for some of 'the cup that cheers but not inebriates' (William Cowper, 1731–1800), although it might be good English, if you don't mind sounding pompous, to make the same request to your host at teatime in the senior common room of an Oxford college.

In the transport café you will get what you want by asking for 'A cuppa char, please' which, if it comes naturally to you, is perfectly good English in that situation, although you would get very low marks if that's what you ask for at a royal garden party.

'Smoking can kill you' is good English. 'Smoking can cause fatal diseases', which is how it appears in some advertising for cigarettes, is not nearly as good. The proof is that advertisers are prepared to spend millions of pounds on advertisements and posters for cigarettes, which have no words on them, sometimes not even the brand name . . . no words, that is, except a warning *not* to smoke! What can we make of this, except that ad agencies are confident that few people will bother to read the stilted phraseology of the warning prescribed by law, even when there is nothing else to read.

It was bad English when this notice appeared in Red Arrow buses in London:

Passengers are requested not to communicate with the driver while the vehicle is in motion.

Now they have changed it to good English:

Please do not speak to the driver while he is driving.

The doors in one Government building still carry this notice:

This door must not be left in an open position.

Some day they will put it into good English—*Please shut the door.*

Even when we have to fax a letter urgently or make a phone call when we're under pressure, we should never lose sight of the purpose of language, which is to move ideas as freely as possible from one mind to another. That is the test we should apply to most of what we write or say.

There are, of course, some exceptions, such as the use of language in creative writing or mysticism. Poetry does not have the obligation to be immediately clear. Sometimes we have to work to sense the imagery of a poet and the reward is an enrichment of our feelings and understandings, an aesthetic experience. The writings of mystics concern a spiritual perception of truth which we may glimpse only in flashes of revelation. When English is used in those ways it belongs to an inner world. But most of us live in the outer world. Here if we make others struggle to understand what we are writing or saying, it is bad English, rotten to the core.

In the 1950s an obscure philologist, Professor Alan C. Ross, carried out a study of the differences between 'upper-class' and 'non-upper-class' English, 'U' and 'Non-U' as it was called. It became fashionable and a surprising number of people still believe in it. Among Professor Ross's 'Non-U' expressions are:

Suit yourself
Don't give up
That's right (for 'Yes')
It's as simple as that
When it comes to the crunch
Believe you me
It's just one of those things
I'll go along with that
Back to square one

Before you drop any of those phrases, because you think they are down-market, remember they're all used in Oxford and Cambridge common-rooms, both Houses of Parliament, the Courts of Law, the White House and from the pulpits of churches.

As for errors in grammar, there's hardly a writer anywhere who has not been picked on for making mistakes. It is a help to be aware of good English usage because when we know the rules we can depart from them with more confidence. But there is no need to be overanxious. Our ear and our common-sense can help us to get through to people and nothing else matters as much.

But here is a warning. Many people are very uptight (*colloq.*) about anything they consider the slightest linguistic mistake. They stay with the rules they were taught twenty, thirty or forty years ago. This is not so much a genuine desire to prevent falling standards as a hardening of the linguistic arteries. But the men and women who are teaching the language now, and who are likely to influence its future development, are much less prescriptive and narrow. In 1988 the National Union of Teachers felt strongly that society needs 'a tolerant, flexible approach to the varieties of English'.

There is scope now for a wider range of personal choice in the use of language and much of the time we can use our feelings and our own judgement to guide us. We are always more likely to get it right when we are sensitive to the circumstances. In a company report, English that seems too easygoing might not inspire confidence. In a letter to a customer, a friendly conversational style might be just the job (*sl.*)

We get through to someone better using words we feel comfortable using and they feel comfortable reading or listening to. There is no need to try to be with it (*sl.*) if that's not your style but a too careful use of language takes all the guts (*colloq.*) out of it.

There are people who are laid back (*sl.*) when they're talking but straighten their tie or put on a tiara the moment they start writing or dictating. Not everyone is comfortable about using, in formal letters, contracted forms such as *I'm, it's, I'll, isn't, can't*. We all use them in conversation but may hesitate to use them in writing in case it's 'wrong'. But as written and spoken English become closer to each other, we see these contractions in more and more official letters from solicitors, MPs, British and American universities and on the leader pages of serious newspapers. Respected novelists, such as William Trevor, Saul Bellow (who won the Nobel Prize for Literature in 1977) and Kingsley Amis (who won the Booker Prize in 1986), use them not only in dialogue but in narrative.

When it seems laboured to write these contractions out in full all the time, the way is wide open now to use *he's, she's, they've* or whatever, when it fits in naturally. If you overdo it, it can sound too casual; but if you always avoid using contractions and spell everything out laboriously, your readers may start to yawn. And you *don't* want that.

It is much the same with so-called *slang*. Many people miss out on good vivid expressions just because they are afraid they're slang, although some of them turn out to be good standard English. There is no fixed rule. You can compare it to clothes; some people wear jeans and T-shirts at the Royal Opera House or at the Metropolitan Opera House while for others anything less than full evening dress would feel wrong.

Before you give up the idea of using a word or a phrase because you think it's slang, just look it up. You might find it was used by Shakespeare and has been in the language for donkey's years (*colloq.*)

The suggestions in this chapter are offered in the spirit of friendliness rather than dogmatism. They are not signposts telling you exactly where to go but a map of the territory to help you find the routes that suit you best. They are based on current usage by good writers, including prize-winning novelists and poets, writers for *The Times*, the BBC and *The New Yorker*.

All changes in the use of English are not for the better and some useful distinctions of meaning are lost on the way. But linguistic history has shown that English has its own instinctive genius, absorbing or rejecting changes as it goes along and still remaining all things to all people in their constant need to communicate. We can all play a part in trying to preserve the best, although it's not always easy to know what the best is, because English has to work for a lot of different people in a lot of different ways. All over the world the language is being stretched in new directions and that is life-giving. W. H. Auden wrote:

Time . . .
Worships language and forgives
Everyone by whom it lives.

The last words can be left to Isaac Bashevis Singer, although his stories are written in Yiddish rather than English. But he was awarded the Nobel Prize for Literature in 1978, so he's worth listening to:

I think the only reason languages disappear is when they lose any creative power.

If that's the case, English is going to be around (*colloq.*) for a long time to come.

Getting through at presentations

If you order elephants or bring on the dancing girls, make sure you relate them closely to what you are putting across.

Everyone who reads this book has to write an important letter at times, or make a crucial telephone call, or argue their way into or out of something. Not every reader is required to make *presentations*, so this special form of communication comes into a chapter near the end. It is not only for directors and executives in business and industry, but for all those other people as well who find themselves dealing with a local committee or stomping round a constituency or a State as part of a political campaign.

If so far such situations have not come into your life, you can leave this chapter until one day, maybe, the time comes for *you* to stand up in a conference room or a committee room, confront a parade of interested or indifferent, receptive or resistant, helpful or hesitant faces and persuade them to buy this, give the go-ahead for that, or accept ideas that mean so much to you.

Why do we spend all this time and money on presentations, instead of leaving it to carefully prepared written recommendations? The reasons are archetypal, a desire deep within us for the directness, immediacy and reality of face to face communication. John May, one of the world's experts on this subject, has defined the purpose of a presentation, which, he says, is:

> To put over to small groups of people, in limited time and differing venues, our facts, figures and ideas by spoken words, aided by visuals, in ways which motivate them to take the action we want.

The last five words are the ones that really count. Do not be misled by the sober grey suits or carefully chosen middle-of-the-road dresses worn by the performers: presentations are a tough hard-hitting business where the sole object is to win. This was demonstrated to the whole world on 8 November 1988. Only two to three months before, Michael Dukakis's lead over George Bush in the opinion polls was in double figures. Richard Nixon, no slouch himself when it comes to presentations, commented on the criticism of George Bush's negative campaigning: 'But if he had been the perfect Texas gentleman . . . all he would have won was a four-year holiday in his summer home in Kennebunkport, Maine.'

We may not feel comfortable with this attitude and might

prefer what Nixon dismissed as a 'kinder, gentler' approach. For some of us there is a line to be drawn, even if the rules of the presentation game are to hit as hard as you can. The head of a London advertising agency did this in his own way when he was presenting a campaign in competition with other ad agencies. It was for a washing powder. He began the presentation by lining up in front of the client half a dozen of the leading brands, including theirs.

'Everything in our campaign, on television and in the press,' he proclaimed 'is designed to do one thing. *This!*' He swept all the products on to the floor, except one. The client was left looking at the product that paid their salaries, their rent and their expense accounts.

Fortunately for the human race, presentations also promote humanitarian causes as well as commercial profit. But the aim of advocacy remains the same, to convince and to win.

Presentations are the theatre of business and taking part in them has something in common with appearing on stage in Shaftesbury Avenue or on Broadway. Actors and actresses go to drama schools: company directors and executives can benefit immeasurably from courses in the art of presentation. Plays are written and rewritten many times and then re-written again in rehearsal: a successful presentation is always the result of writing, re-writing and hours of rehearsal, even if it looks relaxed and informal. Good restaurants may prepare food in advance but every dish looks as if it is cooked fresh for each customer.

The notes that follow take some of the chapter-headings in this book and demonstrate how the ideas can be used to help you *get through at presentations*, which are, after all, another form of communication, peculiarly concentrated and stressful.

Face to face

At a presentation you are face to face with the men and women who can buy your product or services, appoint your ad agency, vote for your party or support whatever other cause you are pleading for. No other form of communication is more demanding and stressful: the decision of the people facing you may be worth thousands or even millions of pounds or dollars to your business. You are likely to be talking to the 'top brass' and, to add to the stress, your own chairman or chief executive may be there listening to you. So much can hang upon how *you* get through.

Everyone is on edge, even if they work hard at not showing it. Your own side want to win and know that they may be up against presentations from competitors. The people at the receiving end want to make the right decision, because a lot may be at stake for them. And this could be your one and only chance, as you are unlikely to be able to make a presentation a second time to the same people.

As we all know, the first problem is dealing with nervousness, as you stand up and the faces in front of you momentarily blur. Smile and welcome the tension as if it were an old friend, because that's what it is. The most experienced actors and actresses feel the same as you do nearly every time they are standing in the wings, waiting to go on, especially on a first night. And a presentation is always a first night. Laurence Olivier is said to believe that if you don't suffer from stage fright just before you go on, you are without talent. A good director may drive an actress to tears to heighten the intensity of her performance. Painful though it is, fear and anxiety can help you come across with strength and purpose. It is useful to recall the advice from an experienced actress in the *Face to face* chapter of this book:

> As I feel my heart beating faster, I concentrate on talking slowly and my nervousness goes or at least it doesn't run away with me.

Tension can help you get the most out of the time you have in front of your prospects and that time is valuable. There is the president of a multinational company who had a special kind of taximeter made for him. At presentations to his board, he feeds in the cost per minute of the people present, based on their salaries. As the meter ticks away, the figure clocking up is daunting and keeps everyone on their toes. When you are facing an audience of that kind, there is no need to be awed, because it is as important to them as it is to you, or they wouldn't be there. But if you bring into mind an imaginary taximeter, you will make every minute count.

The size of an audience should condition the style of speaking. If you lecture to a small group of say ten people or less they will feel they're being hectored. If you are too conversational when you are talking to thirty or more they will feel you are lightweight.

Everyone knows about *eye-contact*. It's in all the books and comes into all the courses. But it often turns out to be no more than a quick glassy look from face to face and that doesn't convince anyone. The better way is to hold the contact a beat or two longer, until there is a mutual awareness of your involvement with each other. Lovers can gaze into each other's eyes for minutes on end. You can't go as far as that at a presentation but good advice to pass on is to look at someone just long enough to take in their features, and then transfer your look to someone else. It sounds commonplace enough but can make a remarkable difference to the flow of communiciation between you and the people listening.

What if something goes wrong? Earlier in this book there was a description of a 'live' television commercial for a cigarette lighter that failed to light on the night. But it didn't turn out to be such a disaster. Blunders can happen no matter how careful we are but they can often be used to win the goodwill of your audience. When a slide was projected upside down at her presentation, the woman presenter smiled and said 'Please don't stand on your head to look at it! It's our job to get it right . . . and that applies to everything else we do for you.' Everyone was pleased and the presentation went on.

When something does go wrong, you have to go into high gear immediately and think fast. Good examples can be inspiring. Here is another one which, like the woman with the upside down slide, actually happened. On stage, in the middle of a tense dramatic scene, the telephone suddenly rang, out of cue. The grand dame of the theatre who was beside it had no choice but to pick it up. She listened for a moment and then passed the phone to the young actress who was also on stage.

'It's for *you*.' she proclaimed.

The young actress was terrified at being landed with the problem but dealt with it like an old trouper. She also listened for a moment or two.

'Thank you for phoning.' she said sweetly, 'But I can't possibly speak to you at the moment.'

She hung up and the scene went on. Nobody in the audience noticed anything amiss, except one man. But then he had written the play.

Getting attention first

In a theatre, the lights go down, the curtain goes up and the attention of the audience is focussed on the stage. It is not set up like that in a conference room. But you can at least cut down on the number of distractions. So often reports are placed on the table beforehand, display material or samples on show. The result is that the conference room itself can upstage the speakers. People giving a presentation are running the show and can dictate the timing so that it gives them as much help as possible: reports can be passed round afterwards and display material or samples can be unveiled at the most effective moment.

Not so long ago, films used to open with credit titles: who produced it, who's in it, who photographed it and so on. As the pace of communication has hotted up, audiences have become more impatient and expect their attention to be grabbed right from the first frame. So most films now begin with a slice of the action. *Crocodile Dundee II* opens with the Australian actor, Paul Hogan, using sticks of dynamite to catch fish from an open boat. He could be back home in the outback of Australia . . . until the camera pans up to reveal he's in New York harbour, with the spectacular Manhattan skyline as a backdrop.

The unexpected is always a good way to get people's attention. Sometimes it can be done just with words. 'I'm in the middle of the most marvellous love affair.' said the chief executive of a company importing fabrics from all over the world, when she opened her presentation to buyers, 'And I'm here to tell you about it.'

They all listened.

'I've fallen madly in love', she went on, 'with the fabulous designs we've found for this spring.'

Sometimes it can be done with drama. A presenter selling his company's security system for retail stores, pointed to the table:

Imagine this table is one of your shops. Our system wraps an invisible infra-red barrier all round it and if anyone tries to break through it, *this* happens!

He picks up an ashtray from the table and a piercing alarm startles the audience. From then on they were with him all the way.

As in those two examples, both from real life, a good presentation should have a sense of showmanship in one way or another. But the razzmatazz of *showbiz* can take over, if it's not well thought out, and can send the audience away singing the songs but forgetting the message. Elsewhere in this book the first Brigitte Bardot television commercial was described. Everyone who saw it remembered her but not so many people could recall the product she was advertising. If you order elephants or bring on the dancing girls, make sure you relate them closely to what you are putting across. Remember how the head of an advertising agency replied to his client's demand for record attention figures:

> Instead of showing a big picture of the car you show a big picture of Marilyn Monroe and a little picture of the car. If that doesn't work, you take some clothes off her!

A stunt can be spellbinding but it is usually only worth it when it helps your message to shine through, as it did when Walter Bentley presented his legendary 8-litre car to the press, by driving it straight up the flight of steps of a London hotel. He made a point that everyone present remembered for the rest of their lives.

The first ten minutes or so of a presentation require the hardest work. You are making contact with the people whose decision matters so much to you, you are setting the tone, you are establishing confidence and authority and you are opening their minds to what you are presenting.

Whatever else you will have learned by heart, you will certainly have learnt the first few sentences of your presentation, if only to give you confidence. But it will come across as more alive and less like the expected sales pitch if you allow it to be a little rough at the edges, as if the thoughts and ideas are flowing through you as you talk. When an attractive woman looks provocatively dishevelled, as if she has just got out of bed, it is often a calculated disorder that has taken a lot of work!

On not boring the pants off them

The more attention people pay to you, the more effective a presentation is going to be. At the same time you cannot expect people to be engrossed in everything you are saying for hours on end. If a presentation starts after lunch, when eyelids are drooping and attention is blurred, or if an audience has already been through other presentations that week, the boredom threshold can be dangerously low.

This is how to tune in to the ebb and flow of attention from the people in front of you. Compare it to the way a good driver is in touch with the engine and transmission of a car, changing gear before the engine labours, anticipating traffic lights, braking before going into a bend and then accelerating to get round it. Like a car engine, an audience can be cold to begin with and we've been looking at ways to warm them up. From then on, you will probably be all right for the next ten minutes or so. After that, attention starts to fall away and that's the moment to change gear.

The structure of a presentation should have different rhythms built in, as a symphony has different movements, a book separate chapters and a play acts and scenes. There are different ways to change the pace of a presentation. Facts can be brought to life by introducing a parable, a form of storytelling that has existed for thousands of years. Not long ago I heard a market research expert wrap his findings in a story that began something like this:

> Three women go into a supermarket. Sylvia is a pretty blonde, about twenty years old, newly married, with no children. Mary is in her mid-thirties. She has a good figure and likes to wear clothes to show it off. She has two children and is married to an assistant bank manager earning £20,000 a year. And then we have Elizabeth. She doesn't like to be called *Liz*, which is not surprising as she is in her sixties. Her husband is retired and they are living on . . .

As he went on to outline their purchasing habits, the people listening found it more human and absorbing than the usual tables of socio-economic groups.

At all levels of sophistication, storytelling can hold an audience. In the arena of the Djemaa el Fna in Marrakesh animated crowds from nearby villages gather round to listen to the convoluted tales from itinerant storytellers. The theatre producer, Peter Brook, kept New Yorkers enthralled in the old Majestic Theatre in Brooklyn, through a *nine-hour* cycle of the Mahabharata, the epic Sanskrit poem, by letting his multi-racial cast recount fables. When rather dull information has to be presented, it is always worth looking to see if it can be embodied in a story.

Visual aids can be introduced to give people something else to look at. But be on guard against putting your audience in the dark while slides or a film are projected, or they might take the opportunity to doze off. You run the same risk if you use visual aids for more than about ten minutes at a time: some people have built up the habit of falling asleep in front of television sets. In any case too many visual aids, no matter how good they are, can be counterproductive, as they can make a presentation lose authority by turning it into a kind of magic-lantern show.

If you really want to see the faces in front of you light up, it's easy: you announce a coffee-break or a tea-break! The showstopper in a great musical on Broadway, *How to Succeed in Business Without Really Trying*, brought the whole cast on to the stage to sing 'If I don't have my coffee-break, something within me dies!' It touched the hearts of the whole audience.

Numerical communication slows down a presentation because unless people are given enough time to understand the significance of figures, they are without meaning. Statistics, percentages, bar charts, graphs and the rest are often essential; and skilfully used, numbers can be as dramatic as words in the communication of ideas. Yet it can be a mistake to assume that everyone listening is as numerate as accountants or computer experts. Unless you are sure of your audience, it is safer to use as few figures as possible and just to build up the *outline* of your case, covering yourself by confirming that the detailed back-up is contained in the report they will take away.

There is one reliable principle that ensures we never bore the pants off anyone. John May, famous for his master classes in business presentation, gives it to us bluntly in six words: *Self-interest is the ear-bender.* We may also believe that people are motivated by love, fellowship, humanity and justice, those qualities that irradiate life on this planet; but at a business presentation you are more likely to succeed if you turn round every proposal you are making so that instead of seeing it your way, you tell everyone who is listening what it will do for them.

How to come to a good end

This is the story of six presentations made by six advertising agencies in New York, who all wanted to win the same account. The chairman of Harvey's, the famous sherry and wine company, had asked me to go to the States with him and two of his directors, to advise on selecting an advertising agency for the American market. Although the account is a modest one by Madison Avenue standards, it is prestigious and six major agencies were interested.

In the first two days we sat through long presentations in the impressive conference rooms of three ad agencies. We were shown an analysis of the pre-dinner drink market, percentages of brand shares, regional breakdowns, readership and television viewing statistics. We came away befogged and weary with figures.

The morning of the third day was different. The presentation lasted only an hour. It opened with the proposition that Harvey's Bristol Cream sherry should be sold as an *after-dinner* drink, since it cost more than most vermouths but less than liqueurs and brandies. The creative head of the agency projected sketches, putting over an idea for a television commercial, and a colour rough for a whole-page advertisement in women's magazines. They were built round a captivating slogan: *Never serve the coffee without the cream—Harvey's Bristol Cream!*

The presentation was over in time for an early coffee-break. Excellent coffee was served in antique china cups. As we were enjoying it a pretty secretary came in carrying a silver salver full of copitas of Harvey's Bristol Cream sherry. 'Never serve the coffee without the cream!' she said disarmingly, as she offered the glasses round.

There were still two presentations to come, from the remaining two advertising agencies, but we had already made up our minds. The most successful presentations are usually as short as they can be, with a central and original idea and a dramatic or human exposition of that idea right at the end.

Most presentations are too long. They are like the windows of cut-price shops, crammed with special offers. Every argument is included, every point is made. And then it is often all repeated at the end in a solemn heavy-going summing up. The old homespun folklore of presentations used to be: 'First you tell them what you're going to tell them. Then you tell them what you're telling them. Last of all, you tell them what you've told them.' Perhaps there is still some truth left in this tired old maxim, even at a time of satellite communication and telefax immediacy. But it can be overdone. We are all aware that solutions to our problems are rarely absolute as there are usually alternatives. Over-emphasis soon becomes oversell and then we walk away.

There is no form of communication in which timing plays such an important part as in a business presentation. There is no form of communication in which brevity is so valuable. And there is no form of communication in which knowing when to stop comes nearer to divine wisdom. It is not uncommon for experienced executives in charge of presentations to have some secret way of telling their team it is time to shut up. A chief executive may take off his glasses, or cross his left leg over the right, or finger the lobe of his ear. Signals like these are used as an order that this is the moment when the clients should have *their* say. People who are half convinced will often do the rest of the work themselves, if they are given a chance.

The most successful way to end a presentation is to break down the *them and us* barrier and bring both sides together in questions and discussion. There is a psychological point when this interchange is most possible but it takes confidence and judgement to stop at that point, to leave the rest of a carefully prepared script unused.

In the next chapter of this book, a professor at Cornell University is quoted on the use of language:

A sentence should contain no unnecessary words, a paragraph no unnecessary sentences, for the same reason that a drawing should have no unnecessary lines or a machine no unnecessary parts.

If we apply all that to every presentation we take part in and work at it, building it into every aspect, we shall be much more likely to come to a good end, with our proposal being accepted, an order being given, a signature added to the bottom of a contract, or at the bottom right-hand corner of a cheque.

Putting it all together

This final chapter draws together all the threads so that we can see clearly the pattern of successful communication. A communication between one person and another can be a living thing or stone-cold dead. This applies in business, politics, personal relationships and in every encounter between one human being and another.

Here is a simple proof of this, carried out by the international advertising agency Foote, Cone and Belding. They made up a batch of the same product in plain white wrappers. Half the wrappers had one slogan on them and the other half carried another form of words. Two packets, each one with a different slogan, were then given away to three hundred housewives.

A week later personal calls were made on every woman and she was asked which of the supposedly different products she liked better. Almost 80 per cent had a positive preference for the product in one of the wrappers. As the two products were identical, only the *words on the packet* could have made such a difference.

If we remember that test every time we write an important letter, pick up the phone or talk to someone face to face, we shall never take for granted the words we use. Choosing the best words so that they lead to the results we want can become a habit, if we work at it. Until then, here is a checklist to keep you on the right track.

1 What do you want to happen next?

This is the most important question about any communication. If it is not asked right at the outset you leave your words to chance. The answer does not always have to be self-seeking; there are times when we want someone to feel comforted, reassured or loved.

In a communication we work backwards from Newton's Law that every action has an equal and opposite reaction. We decide the reaction we want and work back to the words that will produce it.

Faced with a blank sheet of paper, a cassette-recorder or an attendant secretary, it's easy to get obsessed with the question *What do I want to say?* Katharine Whitehorn, the journalist, says that offices and conference rooms 'are jammed with people, half of whom dictate an endless stream of letters and memos and draft documents on to the notepads of the other half, who are secretaries too stunned to protest'.

Everywhere the wastage in wordpower is overwhelming. It is like running an airline with no fixed destinations so you board an aircraft without knowing where it is going to take you. The way out of this is to define the result we want as clearly as possible *before* we start writing or speaking. From that moment on, our words work in an entirely different way.

Alternatives dissipate energy. The human mind needs a definite basis for making a decision and we help someone when our attitude is consistent and positive. When you focus on the results you want, you pick the words that get through for you and leave out all the others.

2 Would you say that to someone you know?

Every story of successful communication has at the heart of it a real contact between one person and another. Ronald Kirkwood, as one of the well-known creative men on the London advertising scene, gave some good advice: 'The best advertisements are those that recognise and take advantage of the opportunity to have a private conversation with someone.'

Before you put a word down, before you go into an interview, before you dial a number, think about the other person. If you are wrapped up in yourself, instead of communicating you are out there on your own.

John Whitney, when he was head of Capital Radio, said he received many letters written as if he were the head of the BBC. Although he tried to deal with all letters fairly, he recollected that he could not help being put off by letters that showed no awareness of the job he was doing, running a lively independent radio station.

It is often a good idea to read your letter out loud to hear what it will sound like to the other person. David Abbott, who became head of his own advertising agency and at one time was said to write the best copy in London, told us:

I always read my copy out loud . . . I often find I'm speaking out loud as I write. Do this and you'll get copy that flows, not to mention a reputation as a moron.

3 Have you made a good start?

It is a basic law in advertising that no advertisement is better than its headline. Tests show that a change in headline can make ten times as many people read the same ad.

Every communication has to start by getting the other person's attention; and the more attention it gets the better it gets through. If we could see a graph of someone's attention, like a cardiograph, as they are listening to us or reading our letter or report, we would work very hard on our opening sentence.

Of course the first thing is to get through to the right person. A lot of advertising is wasted because it is seen by people who would never buy the product. John Wanamaker, who spent a fortune on advertising, once made this classic and rueful quip: 'Half the money I spend on advertising is wasted but I can never find out which half.'

We should always try hard to find out who will take the responsibility to make the decision we require. The bigger the decision, the easier it is to know. The sign on President Truman's desk read *The buck stops here.*

The least we can do is find out the other person's name. 'Dear Sir' or 'Dear Madam' never turned on anyone. Once we know the right person, we've won half the battle the moment we get their attention.

4 Have you bored the pants off them?

How much we can write or say depends upon how important it is to the other person because it is human nature for people to be more interested in themselves than in anything else. John Salmon, the creative director who gave good advice on grammar in the previous chapter of this book, wrote some of the most successful advertisements for recruiting army officers. He wasn't worried, he said, about using a lot of words because 'when you are inviting someone to consider changing their career, they are prepared to read a good deal about it'.

But Edward Heath was given this warning about speaking on television: 'People are not used to hearing speeches in their living room. The same voice talking continuously for more than a minute or two creates a strain.' That's a good reason to avoid making speeches in letters or reports.

For W.H. Auden the severest test of a poem was to write it out in longhand. That can be a ruthless check at times on something we've dictated or typed.

A professor of English at Cornell advised:

> A sentence should contain no unnecessary words, a paragraph no unnecessary sentences, for the same reason that a drawing should have no unnecessary lines or a machine no unnecessary parts.

If we keep to that we are less likely to bore the pants off anyone.

5 Do your words have added value?

Our words always have added value when they appeal to someone's motives and interests. It does not have to be hard sell: it can be done with humour, humanity and warmth and then people respond all the more.

Nearly every outstanding advertisement works because it focuses on one simple idea:

> A group of identical glasses with vodka and chunks of ice in them. One glass is in front. *The words*:
> If Vodka has no taste, how come I can tell which one is WOLFSCHMIDT?

> A picture of a wrinkled, smiling Indian, Western style. He is happily eating a sandwich. *The words*:
> 'You don't have to be Jewish to love Levy's real Jewish Rye.'

> A drawing of a stopwatch with the hand at fifteen seconds. *The words*:
> DON'T WAIT ANY LONGER
> (The Harris/3M fax transmits documents in fifteen seconds.)

If we are anxious about something, it is natural to stress what *we* want and to leave out what it could offer the other person. When a letter is full of *I want* and *I need*, the words drop in value to someone else.

I once saw a copy director turn down an advertisement. 'Tell them what they want to know', he said to the copywriter, 'not what you want to say.'

6 Does the ending do something?

Your last sentence is your last chance to get through. The best endings are action endings. Some ads show a scissors cutting out the coupon. That tells the reader exactly what to do next.

If you are talking or writing to your husband, father, daughter or a friend, your last words can be just as important; they can leave the other person feeling warm and wanted.

The worst endings are non-endings, when a letter or conversation peters out. Try covering up your last sentence. If you don't miss it, you should rewrite it, because your last words can make all the difference.

7 Remember psycholinguistics

Words are loaded with feelings and emotions and can put people off without them knowing why. When you say the same thing in different words, they feel much better about it.

Where possible turn negative statements into something positive. 'We cannot meet your delivery date' is one thing. 'We can deliver for certain by . . . and we hope this will be all right for you' is something else.

We do not always need to spell out in detail all the negative aspects of a situation. People have enough doubts and fears. When there is a dark side, it is better to explain it directly and clearly, rather than camouflage it, and then turn to reasons for hope and encouragement. Winston Churchill was able to do this in the desperate days of the last war.

Remember what happens when confidence in a company is affected: their shares immediately take a tumble. For once, politicians are right when they always talk of winning, even when the odds are against them. Anything can change and 'a week in politics is a long time'.

Words are full of positive and negative energy. So be on guard against using cold words, when it is not necessary. People cannot help being affected by them. Try to replace them by words that are warm and life-enhancing.

8 Have you said too much?

Talking or writing too much conveys uncertainty and insecurity to someone else. When we learn to pause, to be quiet, to write less, our words have time and space to work harder for us.

One of the tests of sentences in advertising copy is 'Do they have people nodding?' We should leave time for the other person to agree, as then they might do half the work for us.

If a letter *looks* too long, it is useful to cover up each paragraph in turn to see if we're better off without it. In every human activity, timing is paramount. Keeping quiet at the right moment can do everything we need.

9 Have you really worked at it?

A successful adman discovered that his son was dyslexic and needed special help at school. The one school that could give him that help was full. Although the boy's father is an experienced writer, he spent a whole week working over his letter to the headmistress. The reply came by return: 'After a letter such as yours, how can I not see you?'

A classic rule in advertising, when it's an important advertisement, is *Hold it for two weeks*. In the States they say that rule can save millions of dollars. It gives someone a chance to think again and do more work on it.

The head of a successful company said 'There are times when even the most brilliant executive must realise that the clever course is not to be clever at all.' It takes time and hard work to be simple.

Most good writers are used to rewriting sentences many times to make sure they are really getting through. Keat's famous line 'A thing of beauty is a joy for ever' first appeared as 'A thing of beauty is a constant joy.' That is not the same line at all.

It's worth going over an important letter again and again. All the effort is worthwhile when it delivers the results you want.

10 Aim to be serious, not solemn

Russell Baker wrote an inspiring piece for *The New York Times*

Magazine. He explained the difference between being serious and being solemn.

As I understand it, being serious is getting through to the heart of the matter. Being solemn is being heavy, laboured and self-important.

Here are some of Russell Baker's examples. Jogging is solemn: poker is serious. 'Once you grasp that distinction', he adds, 'you are on the way to enlightenment.' Among civilisations, he goes on, the Roman Empire was solemn: Periclean Athens was serious. In literature, Shakespeare above all is serious. In journalism, *Playboy* is solemn: *The New Yorker* serious. Among cities, Washington is solemn: New York serious.

To help you get the idea here are some more suggestions. Working out a system to break the casino at Monte Carlo or Cannes is serious: hijacking an aircraft with innocent passengers on board is solemn. A cheese soufflé (when it holds up) is serious: rice pudding must be solemn. Making love can be either serious or solemn: it all depends.

This report from an airline is very solemn:

> We started out with clear research evidence that told us that improvements in the quality of the product delivered to our passengers were not mirrored in the perceptions of those passengers.

It could have been serious:

> We found that passengers didn't know we were doing a much better job.

This headline from an OXFAM appeal is beautifully serious:

> Doing nothing, that's death.
> Helping people, that's life.

Most speeches by most politicians are solemn; even when they are smiling on television, politicians usually manage to look solemn. So it was like a ray of sunshine for the world when in 1985 Mikhail Gorbachev took over as first secretary of the Soviet Communist party. Unlike his solemn predecessors, Khrushchev and Brezhnev, here was a Soviet leader who wore a trilby hat and understood the art of being serious. Life on earth became a little more lighthearted and a Russian word, serious and full of hope, passed into other major languages—*glasnost*.

When we are serious we connect with the mainstream of human experience and feeling. When we are solemn we are out of touch and our words drag. In the 190 or so pages of this book I must at times have lapsed into being solemn. As Russell Baker warns, it is hard to be Periclean Athens and it is hard to be Shakespeare. For that matter, it's not all that easy to make a good cheese soufflé *every* time. It's hard to be serious. But it's always worth trying.

Acknowledgements

The experience, ideas and examples from the work of many people have gone into this book. I am especially grateful to the following:

David Abbott, chairman, Abbott, Mead, Vickers/SMS, London.
Russell Baker, for the theme of his article 'Why Being Serious Is Hard', *The New York Times Magazine*.
BBC, London, for letting me listen to tapes.
Irving Berlin, song-writer.
David Bernstein, The Creative Business, London.
Dr Edward de Bono, for some valuable concepts in his book *Wordpower* (Pierrot Publishing).
British Airways, New York.
Peter Brook, theatre director, for his experience of non-verbal communication and the value of silence.
Roy Brooks Estate Agents: A. R. Halstead, for permission to quote some of the original Roy Brooks advertisements.
Dr R. W. Burchfield, chief editor Oxford English Dictionaries, for comments and a quotation from a letter from H. W. Fowler.
Capital Radio, London.
Henri Cartier-Bresson, for his observation on photography.
Nick Cole, for information about the spread of English, *The Times*.
The late Fairfax Cone.
Alistair Cooke, for many lessons to us all in getting through to people.
Dr Ernest Dichter, founder of the Institute of Motivational Research, New York.
Doyle Dane Bernbach, New York.
Eastern Airlines, Miami.

ACKNOWLEDGEMENTS

Foote, Cone & Belding, London: Brian F. MacCabe, president.
John Georgiadis, leader of the London Symphony Orchestra, for permission to repeat his story about Leopold Stokowski.
Benny Green, for information and comments about Irving Berlin and Cole Porter in *The Listener*.
Professor A. H. Halsey, director of the Department of Social and Administrative Studies, University of Oxford.
Lesley Howard, for valuable comments and help with research.
Douglas Hurd, for information about politicians' speeches, *An End to Promises* (William Collins, Sons & Co.).
The Institute of Practitioners in Advertising, London.
David Jacobs, for taking time to talk and listen to me.
Ronald Kirkwood, Kirkwood & Company, London.
Mary Wells Lawrence, chairwoman, Wells, Rich, Green, New York.
The late Groucho Marx.
John May, who has taught more people (including me) about *getting through*, than he has had hot dinners.
Kay McManus, television and radio writer.
Dr David Mendel, former consultant, St Thomas's Hospital, London, for some advice on 'reading faces', *The Observer*.
Jane Ellen Murray, associate creative director, J. Walter Thompson Company, Chicago, for the title of her article *Would Your Daughter Want to Marry This Ad?*
Iain Murray, for facts about pin-up calendars.
Hubert Nicholson, A. S. J. Tessimond's literary executor, for permission to quote Tessimond's peoms *She* and *Daydream*, included in *Not love perhaps* . . . (Autolycus Press).
David Ogilvy, for comments on *getting through* and some masterly examples of doing it.
OXFAM
The late Eric Partridge, for quotations on slang and reminders of catchphrases in *A Dictionary of Catch Phrases* (Routledge & Kegan Paul).
The Pirelli Calendar Album (Pavilion Books and Michael Joseph).
Joel Raphaelson, editor of *The Unpublished David Ogilvy* (Sidgwick & Jackson, London and Crown Publishers, New York).
Lord Rothschild, for ideas in his lecture *Risk* (BBC).
Bernice Rubens, novelist.
Saatchi & Saatchi: Charles Saatchi, chairman; Len Barkey,

184

deputy managing director.
John Salmon, creative director, Collett, Dickenson, Pearce and Partners, London.
Norman W. Schur, for the schoolboy's description of cricket, *British Self-Taught* (Johnston & Bacon, a division of Cassell).
Isaac Bashevis Singer, writer.
Carlos Slienger, writer and publisher.
Fritz Spiegl, for spotting the quotation from Elizabeth Barrett Browning's letter.
The Right Reverend Mervyn Stockwood, former Bishop of Southwark, for time and advice.
The late John Tessimond, a friend who was a poet and an outstanding copywriter.
Margaret Thatcher, for advice about nervousness and about not quoting too many facts and figures, from her conversation with Kenneth Harris, *The Observer*.
The Times, for some quotations.
Katherine Whitehorn, for comments about problems of communication, from 'Mighty Quill', *The Observer*.
John Whitney, director general, Independent Broadcasting Authority, for giving me time and advice.
Professor Bernard Williams, University of California, Berkeley.
Woolwich Equitable Building Society: Donald Kirkham, chief executive.
The Writers' Guild of Great Britain.
Young & Rubicam, New York and Los Angeles.

Many others in the UK and USA, and some in Australia, have contributed real-life demonstrations of how to use words to get through to people. For these I am also very grateful, because we learn more from actual experience than from anything else. Where appropriate, every effort was made to contact copyright holders and if there are any omissions or inaccuracies, please accept my apologies.

G.H.

Index

Note: Advertisements are grouped together under *Advertisements*, slogans under *Slogans* and television commercials under *Commercials*. *Italic* numbers indicate quotations.

A

Abbott, David, *176*
action endings, 102–4, *179*
Advertisements: American
    Express, 92
  anti-damp spray, 63
  Brooks, Roy, 79–80
  Chevrolet *Camaro*, 95
  Ford cars, 33
  Harris/3M fax, 178
  Hathaway shirts, 93
  investors' newsletter, 62
  London Transport, 61
  Manchester Business
    School, 62
  Norwegian Tourist Office,
    121
  Orbach's department
    store, 63
  Parker pens, 61
  pregnancy advisory
    service, 62
  Rolls-Royce, 83–4
  VD clinic, 62

  Volkswagen, 72–3
  Volvo, 33
  Walls meat pies, 84
  Ziploc sandwich bags, 92
advertising film festivals, 102
Alford, Henry, *147*
Ali, Muhammad, *92*
Alice in Wonderland, *109*
'Americanisms', 149
Amis, Kingsley, 156
applications for jobs, 22–3
archetypes, 117, 122, 161
ASLEF, 119
Auden, W.H., *84*, 152, *157*,
    178
Austen, Jane, *42, 71–2*

B

Baker, Russell, 180–2
Bardot, Brigitte, 59, 166
BBC, 16, 151, 152, 156
Beatles, The, 153
Bellow, Saul, 156
Benson and Hedges, 93

L
Laing, R.D., 89
Larkin, Philip, 152
Lasker, Albert D., *74*
Lawrence, Mary Wells, *55,*
  93
Lawson, Nigel, 121
legal documents, 74
Lennon, John, 21, 153
Lord and Thomas, 103

M
MacArthur, Charles, *108*
Macaulay, Thomas, *141*
Macbeth, *105*
McLuhan, Marshall, *11*
Mahabharata, The, 168
mail-order advertising, 30–1
Man and his Symbols, 47
margarine, 117
Markham, Donald, *96*
Marvell, Andrew, *27–8*
Marx, Groucho, 31
Marx, Karl, 113
May, John, *161, 168*
Mendel, Dr David, *129*
'me too' advertising, 92
Mini, 24, 27
Modern English Usage, 149
Monroe, Marilyn, 58, 166
Morley, Robert, 43–4
motivational research, 87–8
Motivational Research, Institute for, 87
Murray, Sir James, *151*
Murray, Jane Ellen, *39*
Murray, Len, *119*
Murrow, Edward, *134*

N
NASA vocabulary, 149
naturist, 114
nervousness, 131, 163
Newman, Sydney, *129*
Newton's Law, 175
New Yorker, The, 93, 156, 181
New York Times, 180–1
Nixon, Richard, 91, *161–2*
Norman Conquest, 16
nudist, 114
numerical communication,
  77, 168

O
Ogilvy, David, 83–4, *92–3*,
Olivier, Laurence, 163
Olympic Games, 17
Our Town, 64
Oxford English Dictionaries,
  10, 83, 113, 151, 152

P
Packard, Vance, *87*
Partridge, Eric, 10
passive voice, 50
Persuasion, 71–2
Pinero, Sir Arthur, 28, *29*
Pirelli calendars, 57–8
Plato, *75*
Playboy, 181
Porter, Cole, 79
price tickets, 120
Protagoras, *89*
puns, 120
Pure English, Society for,
  149